# BEYOND WORSHIP:

## Meditations on Queer Worship, Liturgy, & Theology

Edited by
JAMES ADMANS

*Beyond Worship: Meditations on Queer Worship, Liturgy & Theology*


For more information contact:
Riverdale Avenue Books
Magnus Books Imprint
5676 Riverdale Avenue
Riverdale, NY 10471
www.riverdaleavebooks.com

Design by www.formatting4U.com
Cover by Scott Carpenter.

Digital ISBN: 9781626016378
Trade ISBN:9781626016385
Hardcover ISBN: 9781626016392

All contributions have been reprinted with the permission of the authors. A smaller edition of this publication appeared as a zine published by the Fort Washington Collegiate Church in 2020, with funding from the Calvin Institute of Christian Worship
First edition, October 2022

## Acknowledgments

I am so grateful for all contributors who made Beyond Worship possible. I would like to acknowledge and extend gratitude to Rev. Dr. Damaris Whittaker, Rev. Michael Vanacore, Dinean Davis, Laurrinda Hatcher, David Ford, Chris Whittaker, Allison Dilyard, Beverley Sheares, Robert Arnau, Melissa Thomas-Baum and the staff and members of Fort Washington Collegiate Church.

I am grateful to Harmeet Kaur Kamboj, Sam Morgan Davis, and Jasmine Rebhun who offered their loving support and feedback behind the scenes.

I am incredibly thankful to Lori Perkins, David Valentin, Alexa Hirsch, and the staff at Riverdale Avenue Books who saw the potential and importance of this project and have spent countless hours to make Beyond Worship possible.

Lastly, additional gratitude to the Calvin Institute of Christian Worship that generously funded the original Beyond Worship zine through their Vital Worshipping Communities Grant that laid the foundation for this publication.

## Table of Contents

# CALL TO WORSHIP & LITANIES

# Welcome!
## By Minister James Admans
### (they/them)

An extravagant welcome to you, my friends, to *Beyond Worship*! My name is Minister James Admans (they/them), and my drag name is Marge Erin Johnson (she/her). I'm a preacher, activist, and drag queen located in New York City.

**What does it mean to be welcoming?**

The term ONA is an abbreviation for Open And Affirming, which is a designation that churches in the United Church of Christ, a mainline Protestant denomination, proclaim that their community is welcoming to all people with particular attention to the LGBTQIA2S+ community.

I write this introduction from the perspective of someone with lifelong involvement in the United Church of Christ. The UCC has just less than a million members in the United States and over 4,000 churches across the country. At the time of writing this section, there are over 1,700 churches in the UCC that have designated ONA status for themselves. Being ONA means being a welcoming congregation, particularly to the LGBTQIA2S+ community that has historically been oppressed by the Church as a whole, but many congregations include other marginalized groups in their ONA statements. Being an ONA church means that the congregation has made a public response and a commitment, usually by congregation-wide vote, to become inclusive and welcoming to queer and trans people so that they may fully participate in the life of the church. Declaring ONA status is also a form of repentance for the Church's historical anti-queer sins. This cultural shift may bring us closer together in community and allow us to grow closer to God.

## Becoming Open & Affirming

Becoming an ONA church is not an easy process even for churches in a denomination that is known for its progressive values, such as the UCC. By utilizing the traditional and often recommended materials, such as those by the Institute for Welcoming Resources, the ONA process can last anywhere from six months to several years. The length of the process depends on the existing culture of the church. Assessments of conflict history and power analysis in communities are considered necessary steps for a thorough process.

Pursuing ONA status is a conversational and covenant-based process. Usually, a team or committee leads a congregation. They assess the values and strongly held beliefs of the church, engage in conversation and theological reflection, and coordinate educational opportunities. Eventually, the team will write a draft of their welcoming statement. This is followed by an exploratory survey that is sent to the congregation to determine whether they would approve the statement via congregation-wide vote. An official vote is not recommended unless the survey yields at least 75-85% responses in support of adopting the statement.

The journey of becoming an ONA congregation is one where the entire community is invested in the process. This includes members who are cisgender and heterosexual. Although becoming an ONA church may start with just a few people, the framing of the process being community-wide is important. Being an ONA church affects everyone in the church, not just the queer and transgender members. The role of an ONA committee or team is leading a church through the process of theologically deciding who they are together and how they will welcome people into their spaces.

## Theological Significance of ONA

The UCC is known to follow the example of Jesus and to be motivated by faith to engage in the pursuit of safety and justice for the "least of these" (Matthew 25:40). Being an ONA church is just one way to work towards that vision through the inclusion and affirmation of LGBTQIA2S+ people. Being ONA is more than just a designation or a title to print on a church sign. Being ONA is a continuous commitment to openness, learning, affirming, inclusion, and being a space of belonging for all people. Continuous learning is especially important. For example, some churches may have become ONA in the '90s and welcomed white cisgender gay men and lesbians without giving much attention to the transgender and nonbinary communities or those who are queer/transgender and BIPOC. A true commitment to ONA requires an ongoing philosophy of cultural humility where the congregation recognizes that there is always more to learn and better ways to engage in allyship.

Many people think of ONA as simply being inclusive. Although being "open" is absolutely part of the journey, one of the common pitfalls of ONA is forgetting about what it means to be affirming. In sum, being affirming means to support, recognize, validate, and encourage queer and trans people in their faith journeys. Additionally, ONA churches must not only minister to the queer and trans community. They must also take into consideration that LGBTQIA2S+ people have contributions that they can make to the church if they choose to do so. Being an ONA church means acknowledging and making space for queer and transgender people to flourish in their faith, which means full participation in the life of the church in its ministries, fellowship, leadership, worship, sacraments, and more. Being limited to openness often means stopping at inclusion, which can lead to assimilation into cisgender and heterosexual church culture. Being affirming allows for a reshaping of the overall church identity and a reevaluating what it means to be in community together. Being affirming requires centering the voices, theologies, and justice concerns of the LGBTQIA2S+ community.

## Bring In *Beyond Worship!*

*Beyond Worship* came to fruition after Fort Washington Collegiate Church (FWCC) made the Spirit-led decision that the church needed to live into what it means to be Open and Affirming (ONA). Fort Washington Collegiate Church has been an ONA church for many years. They hold both ONA and "Room For All" designations—RFA being the equivalent of ONA in its dual denomination, the Reformed Church in America (RCA). FWCC has had queer ministers, marched in the Heritage of Pride Parade in New York City, hosted monthly queer theology bible studies, and had a thriving LGBTQIA+ ministry called Beyond Labels. When the leaders and ministers at Fort Washington Collegiate Church came to the realization that we still had more work to do, we applied for a grant through the Calvin Institute of Christian Worship. We were already open, and in many ways, we were affirming. Nonetheless, we found a need to be on the growing edge of what it means to be an ONA congregation. So, we queered the church's heart and center—our weekly Sunday worship, in the hopes that it would have ripple effects throughout our church and the neighborhood.

*Beyond Worship* was originally an online zine with 11 contributors funded by a Vital Worshipping Communities Grant through the Calvin Institute of Christian Worship. This was one of FWCC's various projects using this grant funding, among others, such as starting a drag ministry, bringing in a number of queer and transgender preachers and speakers, and organizing a transgender allyship training. The original Beyond Worship zine was published with the intent to invite authors to participate in our Sunday worship with the hopes of centering their voices and theologies. Additionally, the zine sought out those whose theological voices may often go unheard. Over half of our authors were young people and from the transgender and nonbinary community, with very few being ordained.

This version of Beyond Worship is an expansion of the original online zine with more than double the original contributions. All pieces are written by members of LGBTQIA2S+ community and are from a variety of different faith traditions, although it is necessary to recognize that most are Christian. I find the words and faith journeys of these authors to be deep and powerful, and I believe with that the Holy Spirit used her queer magic to bring these pages together. In a society that often seeks to invalidate LGBTQIA2S+ people of faith, I am thrilled to know that these authors have a space to share their words, gifts, talents, and wisdom.

The structure of this anthology is similar to a worship service. You will find five sections: 1) Calls to Worship & Litanies, 2) Prayers, Poems, & Songs, 3) Testimonies & Sermons, 4) Responses & Rituals, and 5) Benedictions. You are invited to read and move through this book as you would experience a typical worship service. You may read it in order in one sitting or out of order in many sittings. Alternatively, you may read sections or individual pieces as you feel called to do so. Although these pieces are organized into categories, we as queer people are often called to be disruptive towards categories. So, my hope is that you go forth reading and reflecting as you wish. You are also invited to share these pieces with your own faith communities, especially in worship. If you decide to do so, please include printed attribution to the original author(s) and to *Beyond Worship*.

Queer theory tells us that queer and transgender people have always been around, and we always will be as long as humanity is in existence. Likewise, queer and trans people of faith have always existed and will always exist. From a Christian perspective, I believe that we are all children of God, wonderfully made, unique and different on purpose. There is so much more to faith beyond our typical worship spaces that can be limiting, especially when queer and trans people have been forced to the margins. That is why it is so important to have pieces like those presented here in *Beyond Worship*.

* * *

## References

"UCC Open and Affirming Coalition," UCC Open and Affirming Coalition, https://openandaffirming.org/.

UCC Center for Analytics, Research & Development, and Data, "A Statistical Profile 2020 with Reflection/Discussion Questions for Church Leaders," https://uccfiles.com/pdf/2020statisticalreport.vfw.pdf.

Open and Affirming [@UCCcoalition], Tweet, *Twitter*, June 24, 2022, https://twitter.com/UCCcoalition/status/1540333931123204096.

"Beyond Worship Zine," Fort Washington Collegiate Church, https://www.fortwashingtonchurch.org/beyond-worship-zine.

## Litany of Hell and Back
## By Rev. Dr. Mary Barber
**(she/her)**

Gracious, loving creator, nonbinary parent, source of life and breath,
We gathered here want to say,
We have been to hell and back.
*We have been to hell and back.*

We have been to hell and back.
*We have been to hell and back.*

With more than two years of lock-down, shut-down, hunker-down, and just being down
*We have been to hell and back.*

With construction noise pounding day and night outside our homes and classrooms
*We have been to hell and back.*

With Greek letters we never thought would be applied to something that is attacking our bodies, delta and omicron and omicron's evil twin
*We have been to hell and back.*

With something like a little paper mask becoming a major political issue
*We have been to hell and back.*

With anti-trans laws being sold as protecting children when they will literally kill children
*We have been to hell and back.*

With telling about our history, the recent past as well as the more past-past being trashed and banned and spun into a boogeyman theory when it is simply the truth
*We have been to hell and back.*

When Black men and women and Black trans women are still getting killed in our streets but our media and our workplaces and our churches are just trying to get back to "normal" so we can't keep paying attention to that
*We have been to hell and back.*

Yes, we have been to hell and back, Divine Diva, Most Holy One.

We need your help. Help us. Heal us.
*Help us. Heal us.*

We need your nonbinary, Black and all colors fabulousness to show yourself.
*Help us. Heal us.*

Heal us from our exhaustion.
*Help us. Heal us.*

Heal us from this constant barrage of bad news and bullshit.
*Help us. Heal us.*

Heal us from our own distraction and willful ignorance.
*Help us. Heal us.*

Bring us to a new place, help us help you with that new thing you are creating.
*Help us. Heal us.*

Bring us back from hell. Amen.

* * *

**Rev. Dr. Mary Barber (she/her)** is a queer Episcopal priest living in New York's Hudson Valley (Munsee Lenape land) and serving at two churches. She and her wife are parents of two adult daughters. Prior to entering ministry, she worked as a psychiatrist at a state hospital.

## Our Queer Gifts to the Church
**By Jory Mickelson**
**(he/they)**

*do you know what it's like to live*
*someplace that loves you back?*

–Danez Smith, form "Summer, Somewhere"

What is the church? Where is the church? For so many years, it has been a museum, a place to display the traditions and beliefs of previous generations. "Look how beautiful this is," someone says. "My grandfather built that," someone replies. But now the museum is falling into disuse; it has so few visitors. The museum is quickly becoming a mausoleum: an impressive building to house a tomb. But Christianity is the story that pivots on an empty tomb. For generations LGBTQIA2S+ people have not been admitted to the museum, and only recently some denominations have begun to hand out tickets. "Come and see," we are told. But we are a people who have grown beyond welcome, beyond affirmation. We are a people who have stepped out of the cold of the tomb and into the warm caress of the living world. The prophetic word that LGBTQIA2S+ people bring to the church today is, "He is risen!"

Christ is risen from the tombs of strangers' gossip, the shame of our families, and the condemnation of religious institutions. Christ is risen in the truths we dare to speak aloud, in the justice we demand, and in the bodies we remake for ourselves. Christ is risen despite how we are beaten, oppressed, and even killed. Christ is risen, and present in the midst of our celebrations, our loving and sorrow, and our excess. Queer people affirm to the church that Christ is truly risen and is to be found in the world, beyond the beautiful walls of empty churches, beyond the quiet graves they are quickly becoming. LGBTQIA2S+ people proclaim to the church today that Christ is risen, indeed—wherever truth is being lived out and there is loving between people. We speak with the angel at the tomb on Easter morning saying, "He is risen from the dead and going ahead of you..." To find him, we must take the next step.

Queer people's gift to the church is one of rupture and disorder. LGBTQIA2S+ people rupture the silence of what God's people fear to speak aloud and attempt to hide away, rupturing our private spiritualities into a public faith and the barrier that church walls have become and lets in the world. LGBTQIA2S+ people bring a gift of disruption, like the earthquake that came to Peter in prison, which lets us out of our prisons and into the world. A radical shaking up that shows us that God is indeed present in real human bodies as well as outside of our churches and is the mud and mess of the world. Amid the trashiness, excess, sin, brokenness, riots, revelry of our lives.

LGBTQIA2S+ people bring the gift of their own lives to all of God's people, lived out daily in authenticity and truth. Despite injustice. Despite oppression. Despite violence and death on a daily basis. Despite the world's continual "No." But as physician Dr. Gabor Maté says, "Safety is not the absence of threat... it is the presence of Connection."

It is in the truth, in the virtue of LGBTQIA2S+ people's lives lived in authenticity that they find both their community and resilience. In our very existence, we discover and bear witness to God's people to the overflowing love that wipes away every obstacle and opposition.

By our very breath, we show God's people, as God's people that it is possible to DANCE when it seems the whole world we relied upon is burning down around us. When nothing seems certain. Even when it appears we are in the middle of the end. That in fact, God calls us to celebration and praise, and to dance and leap with joy at the end. Because it is not actually the end—is not death at all, but resurrection.

LGBTQIA2S+ people show that God's love has not been lost. That the Loving One has not gone down to the grave and remained. But is risen indeed. Because the whole story pivots on an empty tomb. Sorrow turned to joy. We have been returned like the coin that was lost and is indeed worthy of celebration, or an entire parade.

Queer people proclaim to the church again and again that the Love of God and Jesus are making themselves known to us. But it is, in fact, already fully-present in our midst. God's "Yes" is both in the present and forever. Our love is but one small part of that great overflowing, a love that gathers us all in, gathers us all together into the very kin-dom of God.

*Adapted from an essay for Extraordinary Lutheran Ministries (ELM), 2022*

* * *

**Jory Mickelson (he/they)** is a queer, nonbinary writer whose first book, *Wilderness/Kingdom*, is the inaugural winner of the Evergreen Award Tour from Floating Bridge Press and winner of the 2020 High Plains Book Award in Poetry. They are the recipient of fellowships from the Lambda Literary Foundation, Winter Tangerine, and the Helene Wurlitzer Foundation of New Mexico, and are a 2022 Jack Straw Writer in Seattle, Washington.

## Liturgy for the Spiritually Confused
## Words of Comfort for the Queer Ex-Evangelical, Former Fundamentalist, and Proud Pentecostal
## By Shaun McCaulla
**(he/him)**

**Liturgy for the Spiritually Confused**

- Words of Comfort for the Queer Ex-evangelical, Former Fundamentalist, and Proud Pentecostal

**Introduction**

Being Jesus Christ's "warrior" agreed with me once, but I have grown to like the term Christ's "lover" better. I've traded in swords for flowers, shields for an open heart, and helmets for a Third Eye so that I may give, receive, and perceive the mystery that is all around. I denounce your "war" metaphors and your "Battle Cry." They are moot, and your certainty is irrelevant. Have you experienced God's presence? Have you been touched by the Divine? It is all that I need to know that life is brimming with the unexpected and it is calling me to discover its wonders.

**Shame**

- You are exactly who you are meant to be.

Please hear me when I tell you: you are not broken.
Please hear me when I tell you: you have not disappointed God.
Please hear me when I tell you: you are not being tempted by Satan or the Devil.

You are made by God, you are valued, you are human, and you are extraordinarily loved.

* * *

Goodbye to shame.
    Hello to accepting my body.
Goodbye to homophobia.
    Hello to waving a rainbow flag.
Goodbye to hiding in the closet.
    Hello to nurturing my inner light.
Goodbye to toxic savior complexes.
    Hello to acceptance from my community.
Goodbye to strict obedience.
    Hello to living in the moment.
Goodbye to feeling bad about sex.
    Hello to healthy intimate relationships.
Goodbye to religious certainty.
    Hello to the mystery of being alive.
Goodbye to the church I once considered family.
    Hello to the people who love me just as I am.

**Loneliness**

- You are surrounded by love.

Tiny Affirmations for the Broken-hearted

- You have not lost; you have gained.
- You have gained a glimpse of yourself that has never been nourished, that has never been cared for.
- You found it; you found a new piece of you.
- Keep finding more when you can; even when the voices that tell you that "you aren't" or "you can't." Don't let them stop your discoveries.
- You are always more than what you think you are.
- God delights in your findings; you have just started to explore.

- You are loved even when you don't feel like it.
- You are held even when the hands that once held you resist touching you; they don't know what they are missing.
- May you be filled with hope; may you find places to name who you are.
- I am lesbian.
- I am gay.
- I am bisexual.
- I am transgender.
- I am queer or questioning.
- I am intersex.
- I am asexual.
- I am who I am.
- Amen.

**Confusion**

- You know more than you think you know.

- Have I disappointed God?
- You are held by the light, by the Earth, by your own compassion, by the Divine, and by God, however you wish to name Them.
- Let yourself be confused. Let yourself doubt. But don't beat yourself down—you are too precious.
- They have created their god to stop you from flourishing.
- But your God calls you home. She calls you to love and be loved.
- Go and be loved while you doubt; embrace the mystery with a warm hug.

**Joy**

- You have the capacity to flourish.

Lift your hands.
Cry out loud to music that moves you.

Speak in tongues if you feel moved.
Don't let them take away your Spirit.
Praise God in the ways that make your body feel good.
These actions are not exclusive.
They are yours.

Carry them with you:
For comfort.
For joy.
For strength.
For a gentle reminder that you are never alone.

Allow them to change if it feels right.
Tap into the actions that you haven't visited in a while.
See what they feel like.
Notice if they bring up memories you would rather forget.
Notice if they bring up memories you cannot live without.

Your body will know because it has always known.
Trust your queer instincts and know that you are loved.

Amen.

* * *

**Shaun McCaulla (he/him)** is a Master of Divinity candidate at Union Theological Seminary, concentrating in LGBTQIA+ Spiritual Care. He is exploring queer identity through the lens of being raised in an Evangelical, Christian Fundamentalist, and Pentecostal community and finding his path as a gay spiritual care leader in New York City and beyond. Shaun lives in New York City with his partner Raymond (he/him) and their two dogs, London (she/her) and Fred (she/they).

## A Litany for Participating in our Own Creation

**Chloe Specht, M. Div.**
**(she/they)**

LEADER: God of Creation, we are your children — bearers of your divine image.
You formed us in your likeness and made us creators just like you are.

**ALL: Loving Creator, invigorate our creativity.**

God, you have called us your own, and we have called you ours.
You beckoned us into being at the beginning, and you beckon us into being still today.

**Loving Creator, remind us that we are sacred,**
**and empower us to participate in our own creation.**

God our Mother, this world is your womb,
and here we are growing, forming, and expanding in your holy mystery.
You are creating alongside us; you are creating with us.

**Loving Creator, embolden us to be midwives of ourselves.**

God, in this life we encounter people who tell us who we should be and try to force us into boxes we don't fit in.
May we remember the person we are deep in our soul.
Let us hold on to the truth that we are beloved and we belong.

**Loving Creator, fill us with holy imagination**
**as we create the person we are becoming.**

God, pour your lovingkindness into our hearts so that we may
celebrate the uniqueness within ourselves and others.
Let your unconditional love radiate in us and through us.
May the good news of your liberation ripple throughout the cosmos!

**Loving Creator, hear our prayer. Amen.**

* * *

**Chloe Specht (she/her), M.Div.** is a queer, autistic theologian. She's passionate about creating inclusive, liberating spiritual communities and is a candidate for pastoral ordination in The Christian Church (Disciples of Christ). Connect with them on Instagram and Twitter at @chloejspecht.

# PRAYERS, POEMS & SONGS

## Today I Felt Like Dying
**Chris Curia**
**(he/they)**

today, I felt like dying
knowing I would just be lying
to myself here and to you now
if I didn't know or name the ways
this pain still runs its course
this death still courses through our veins
in ways, the thing still brings me to tears

year after year after year

and of course, of course it did
and of course, of course it still does
this heart's walls run thin and coarse
chaffing against every goddamned thing
we've had to hold since two days before
wondering where and when it all went
and how much time passed
and what the hell even happened—

now, hold up
whatever happens next
let this cup pass through
no empty threats of shattering graves
or naming hopes you know weigh heavy

say your peace to honor what you need
then endure long enough to become

today, I felt like dying
wondering if all this was really living
and going through the hells that raised us
meant love would conquer everything
holding our breath to breathe our last
might tell us what in god's name we do
with the time supposedly given to us

year after year after year

so we wait, and maybe this is all there is
if so, maybe we just let our crooked hearts
run rampant with time to kiss and tell
everything comes to a head this way
conceding, this is just where it all ends
pack our overnight bags, count our losses
dig our graves and pay our respects
pass the peace to lovers long gone—

now, wait just a minute
I cannot ignore something I have been told
something stirring in me, even now
tells me there must be something more
even in this unknowing we cannot go back
to who or what we thought we wanted
or who we thought we might become

today, I felt like dying
because I'm not so sure
about this whole living business, you see
there's already too much that is left to lose
by the way, plotting graves is a losing game

sometimes love cannot conquer everything
sorry to put to death this fever dream

over and over and over again

so here I am, surrender
not because I am brave, mind you
but because I am tired and weary
and you said come and I said give me rest
just one place to lay this feeble, fickle head
any grave or empty tomb will do
I don't even need a fanfare
just a welcome home, child—

now, look, you've been gone a while
heralding the dark in the gloom
and up here, all hell breaking loose
and turning into something new, whatever
we're glad you conquered death and all
but we're all so proud of you for leaving
growing into what you would become

that was the day you felt like dying
so here's to everything left unsaid
who on earth or what the hell really knows
what could even happen next
if the thought terrifies your insides
join the fun, you'll soon realize
we're all just dying in the end

over and over and over again

across these flickering, faultless stars
lying within some lovers' arms
is where I learned that love was in me

and you and us all the time, all along
holding each other so close as we watch
our dreams firework into twilight
shimmering darkness, death has a name
everything came, coming to its end—

now, we need an epilogue for this ending
empty graves don't tell the whole story
when bodies break long before they rise
returning us here, now, to oohs and ahhs
one last miraculous breathing our last
perhaps this is where we begin again
right by our graves, pierced in the sides

today, I feel like dying
shooting stars and contrite hearts
no need to hide our holy hands
as they intertwine, hold me close, let me go
and tell me when you do, I love you
of course this means to be alive
is to come and die as we become

all we are over again

* * *

**Chris Curia (he/they)** is a graduate student in Seattle studying theology and psychotherapy. In addition to their work in spiritual communities and their various written publications, they also curate a podcast called Through the Darkness. Stay up to date with Chris' work on socials @chriscuringle.

## Neshama Amukah (Deep Breath)
**Elana Naomi**
**(she/they)**

* * *

Poem was reformatted for publication, to see original version go to instagram.com/elana.naomi

Being queer feels as inherent and liberatory
as being Jewish.
Both anchored deep in my soul,
reflections of each other,
teaching me about love and community,
about justice - Tzedek.
I know the universe is expansive
and that there is Good to be found in every being.
I feel something shift in my chest,
            roots flow through the soles of my feet
when I enter my synagogue and sit in the pews.
When I put my tallit around my shoulders,
I remember braiding my father's tzitzit during the High Holidays,
before I had my own.
            There is something beautiful and everlasting
about Judaism -
the way we put stones on our loved ones' graves
instead of flowers,
the way we celebrate the trees,
the way we have continued from generation to generation
            - l'dor v'dor.
Being Jewish
            has shown me the magic in the mundane,
in lighting candles, in flowing water, in the trees,
in my grandmother's matzah ball soup
and my Bubbe's brisket.
We are all fragments of the universe;
            I know my queerness and my Judaism go hand in hand,
            the way they both celebrate liberation,
            and emet - Truth.

## *Beyond Worship*

Being queer feels as inherent and liberatory
as being Jewish.
Both anchored deep in my soul,
reflections of each other,
teaching me about love and community,
about justice - Tzedek.
There is a comfort, in constantly learning
and unlearning,
an endless motion to queerness,
the ceaseless tides
roots flow through the soles of my feet
connecting me to the same dirt that my queer,
Jewish elders were made of -
the same dirt we will return to.
From ashes to ashes,
dust to dust.
It is holy to experience a love so divine.
There is something beautiful and everlasting
about queer community, our chosen families,
our willingness to go beyond what we were taught was
love and relationality.
To embrace with arms wide open, to see one another for our deepest
selves, and love, and love, and love.
Being queer
has shown me the magic in the mundane,
in laughing so hard it hurts, in button down shirts,
in sex at 4pm on a weekday,
for longer than we should.
I know my queer body and love are b'tezlem elohim
- in the image of god.
I know my queerness and my Judaism go hand in hand,
the way they both celebrate liberation,
and emet - Truth.

**Elana (she/they)** is a queer, Jewish, abolitionist who loves poetry, the color green, and her radical, queer community. She's the co-founder of the Jewish organization Making Mensches (@makingmensches and makingmensches.com) and Tu BiShvat is their favorite Jewish holiday. You can find Elana at @elana.naomi on IG and @elipkin6 on Twitter.

## A Whole New Theory of the Universe
## By Lou Nelson
### (they/them)

We receive grace as a picked apart home
yelling to each other in untended wildflowers
        The weapons of mercy can be potent.
my body was
        a despised Samaritan—
          a "female problem"
        Already "unclean"
it kept drifting away from a hidden world of beauty,
        unwilling to risk contamination from a loss of moral sense
looking for a way to kill the scandal of all living things.

lostness really is
Returning home
        God's love and forgiveness
the zigzag paths of dragonflies

Gradually, very gradually, I fell in love.
It felt exactly like a celebration.

*Format adapted for print. Originally composed as a collage of phrases excised from an evangelical Christian lifestyle book.*

* * *

**Lou Nelson (they/them)** is a transmasculine writer and recovering missionary kid. Spreadsheet geek by day and collage poet by night, they create poetry out of whatever they can find around them.

## A Prayer That Comes to Me as I Stare Down the Road

**By Petra Totten**
**(she/they)**

While I drive on the interstate—headed west—I can't help but think on the unseen and violent histories inherent within the landscapes yawning before me:

They're here, written in the land.
(on its body)

What acts have transpired, what rules created to diminish the light and the life that has been given to each of us? Histories of bodies being governed and moved about. All this is written on the body of the land, which leads me to wonder…

What is written on my body?

Depending on your belief, my spirit (soul)
        my intelligence (mind)
          my essence; (presence)
            my aura (energy) is housed within this body.

I see my body and others see my body. I see it as only I can.

It's a feminine body.
(a masculine body)
It's shorter than most others I see.
(a bit wider)

Where is my body?
(my body is here)
How is my body?
(what space does it take up?)

In my mind, I create a list. A list of places; places where gender doesn't matter:

in nature    my professor's office    my high school's theatre    in my car

while I'm riding my bike,    in my garden,    on a trail,
        in my bed

These places make up who I am, and I see myself reflected in the space I take up, and in the space I leave behind.

This prayer is a hope for the future,
a reminder of the connections we feel inside and of the love a Creator has bestowed upon us.
A love that is infinite, that is not burdened by history, by circumstance, of biology or situation.

It is offered at all times and in all places.

May I do likewise, to myself and to those whose space I share.

* * *

**Petra Totten (she/they)** is an Emmy Award-Winning filmmaker and video artist currently based in Toronto, Ontario. Their work has been screened in galleries and festivals in Asia, Europe, and North America. Peter's work is exploratory in nature, seeking to highlight the beauty in lived experience; utilizing the essay film form and visual anthropology to represent communities in ways grounded in care and mutual respect.

## Saints Among Us

**By Natalie Smith**

**(she/her)**

*For Emma Wonsil and Rome*

I dubbed you the gay virgin
Oh patron saint of defiance
Oh saint of endurance
watched you exist in a world that denied the truth of you
wondered how you kept going
when every mass
every theology class
your two-hour confession
told you to be someone else
to silence your sainthood
to deny love
deny all that's holy and sacred
You of the Dog Voice
You of the always has a book on hand
bookmarking your book with another book
certain there's a grape in your drink
Always reaching in
sticky all over the bar counter
I hope you always have bread on your table and hot pockets in your freezer
Oh woman mosaic
Oh decorative snap backs on the wall

Oh spray-painted record player
Oh fighter of the good fight
Oh mixer of sacred and profane
They say I can't nominate a living saint
yet in my own company of holy ones
You're already canonized

* * *

**Natalie C. Smith** is a visual and spoken word artist as well as poet. She works as a mail carrier for the United States Post Office. When Natalie is not delivering mail or turning over words and phrases in her head, she spends her time outside climbing mountains in Colorado. She lives there with her fiancée and an untold number of houseplants.

## A Queer Phos Hilaron:
## An Evening Prayer for Lighting the Lamps
**By Allison Dilyard**
**(she/her)**

Joyous, jovial, jubilant light – gayest light!
Glistening with the glory of God,
 burning with boundless love,
 forever reflected in you and me and everything in between.
Blessing humankind by becoming human so that humankind can be blessed, to bless itself beyond space and time.

Inimitable yet infinitely intimate,
 a vision of our Creator, in every visage.
 Our Creator who ceaselessly re-creates,
 perpetually perfects the Universe to be
 holy, hallowed, heavenly–blessed.
Blessing humankind by becoming human so that humankind can be blessed, to bless itself beyond space and time.

And now that we arrive at sunset's circadian observation,
 beholding that uneclipsable light–
 we hymn to, we sing to, we praise
 the consummate Being of being,
 simultaneously singular and inestimable,
 with the Spirit's sacred breath.
Blessing humankind by becoming human so that humankind can be blessed, to bless itself beyond space and time.

For that breath—our breath—
That Spirit—our Spirit—
is always, eternally worthy
to be the inspiration and aspiration
of songs and poems and prophecy and everything in between.
Blessing humankind by becoming human so that humankind can be blessed, to bless itself beyond space and time.

Lauding loudly all of Your beloved blessings,
glistening in the gilded glow of evening's golden hour,
we know that we are alive
because we know that You are alive,
Blessing humankind by becoming human so that humankind can be blessed, to bless itself beyond space and time.

*Amen.*

* * *

**Allison Dilyard (she/her) is** a Lutheran Lesbian who wears many hats, both literally and figuratively. Currently, she composes craft coffee concoctions for the denizens of Inwood and Washington Heights (NYC) for a living, but has been known to be a professional dilettante, having preached the Gospel, ministered to youth, peddled luxury goods to mind-bogglingly wealthy tourists, wrote piffle for Paulists, and educated and encouraged struggling college students. She received her BA in religious studies from Barnard College, writing an exhaustive thesis about socially transformative Christian mysticism. She then went across the street to get her M.Div. from Union Theological Seminary, where she focused on biblical philosophy and studied the concept of glory (chabod/doxa). The self-proclaimed Viscountess of Seaman Avenue, Allison lives in Uptown Manhattan with her Presbyterian partner, Marranda, their multitudinous fickle houseplants, and their ornery-yet-affectionate pet rabbit, Bunhoeffer.

# Selections
## By Ash Rowan
**(they/he)**

### G(RADIANCE)

God was not satisfied to create the light and the darkness in binary absolutes only. We exist in, and on, a spectrum of infinite chromatics. Continuums of visible and invisible threads woven together form the expansive fabric of our universe. Surely, our Maker delights in that diversity of Their creating: the whole and varied eternal progression of it, and every glorious degree.

## PRAYER FOR & FROM THE ROAD TO EMMAUS

*First given 17 October 2020 for the LDS Emmaus ministry*

Our Mother / Father / Creator-God, who is in heaven, and who is with us: we have been blessed to gather in this space together as Your children. We seal this meeting up unto you. We dedicate it, and the words which have been spoken; we dedicate our very hearts, our minds, our lives, our selves, and our be-ings to do the work which Christ has shown to us, and follow the path which He walked (and has invited us to also join Him in walking). We walk that road to Emmaus together.

MotherFatherGod, please give us a measure of Your Spirit of Love, that we may be bolstered and comforted; that we may know how best to serve. That we can have eyes to see, and ears to hear the cries and calls of those who are seeking help that we can give. Help us administer to them, and to each other. We know that with Your help, we can gather everyone in, every single lost sheep.

We love You, and ask for this consecration in the sacred, holy name of Your Son, our Savior, our Jesus. Amen.

## On the Mount of Trans-figuration

I climb the mountain, alone:
hand
        over hand
and foot
        over foot,
with no one greeting me at the summit but
birdsong and breeze.

God whispers my new name into the morning mist,
that by which I shall be known.
calls me son, child,
as I offer up my body for sacrament upon Their altar
        (Their surgery table)—
weeping, begging, to be fixed.

dawn's light overflows into every valley,
and that of my cavernous ribs.
I am blessed, and newly broken,
molded, like wet earth
into something greater.
but God,
        oh, God,
          *it hurts.*

I sleep,
and I wake:

aching, raw,
fingertips tracing over new scars
like the ones borne by my Brother
in hands
    and in feet;

our new bodies
    new selves
can never be what they once were—

*isn't that the point?*

my chest burns
and, with a smile, I exhale.
I climb down the mountain, alone.

* * *

**Aisling "Ash" Rowan (they/them, he/him)** is a bird buff, general enthusiast, and aspiring fossil, who advocates for fully inclusive celebration of the infinitely diverse ways of being human. Describing themself as "liminally Mormon" and a Unitarian Universalist, Ash strives to emulate the devoted discipleship and radical kindness of Fred Rogers, and seeks Truth and light wherever it may be found. Ash Rowan currently lives with his spouse and sprogs in the valleys of Utah, where magpies sing about home.

## 7 Psalms
**Joshua David Murphy**
**(they/he/she)**

i awoke this morning with a prayer.
<<take me to the internal.>>
It is here where I will reside with you
In between my lungs
The place that burns
Longs and even cries

Be still

I have been told that there are 7

7 sacraments
7 tribes
7 chakras
7 elevens

It is here where I pause and tell you

<<this is not a joke>>

7 is the key to humanity
7 is a reminder
Of communion
And conversation
Oneness

<<me, you>>
<<us>>

Us is the oneness we crave
To be seen, heard, and live together
As One

Me sharing the best of me
You sharing the best of you
Withing our lives
Together

7 opportunities
For you to die
And be revived

As an avatar in a simulation
A warrior learns from their mistakes or dies by them
It is your chance.
Do you learn?
Do you grow?
Do you change
Do you evolve
Or go back to how things used to be
Until you get it right.

You have a responsibility to yourself to experience the 7 sacraments within you
Chakras you can always channel.
And have a conversation with.

Die and try again
From the moment you wake
To the moment you are asleep

Who am I in this period
Who am I in this semicolon
<<this is not a joke>>

I was a lifetime.
And you are too.

We connected then
And never let go of one another.

How do we keep listening to one another
And learn more about each other
Treating each other
As if they were our ancestors
Hoping to have us learn from their sacred lessons

+

There is a river
That is big enough
To wash away all our sins
All our inequities
Cleanse us of our ambition
Our greed
Our power
Our oppression
For our closed minds
And bloody fingers

To restore
To refresh
To begin again
When your toe touches the shore
And you begin your next life again.

We are each logs
Traveling down The River of Life
Until we break
And return together
In one big ocean
Into One Love

Oneness.

++

Where everything exists freely in harmony and balance with one another.

I like to imagine the best and alternate versions of one another.
We are each meeting each other with the lessons we'd like to learn for ourselves.
To help others.

How do we pray for others to have the chains that bind them broken.
That was you in a previous life
Or perhaps an emotion you felt manifested
Do you believe
Do you receive
The eucharist of Life?
The light within us all?
The fire that binds us
That was stolen and given to us
To share among each other
Our resources

Competition is our greatest enemy
The game must end.
Acknowledge and assess our issues.
And help each other deal with them.

+++

John and Jesus were just men who agreed
A confirmation is just an oath that you believe in something greater than yourself.
John and Jesus were just men who agreed that One was Divine.

++++

Every human emotion.
Scared
Anxious
Overwhelmed
Peaceful
Lustful
Lazy
Eager
Ambitious

How do I fight a power of oppression?
Just be cool.

Thoughtful
Intentional.

Don't worry
Be happy

Fight the power

+++++

A prophet on the beach once said
To love is to be in the very heart of God
Big love unites us.

We have been taught
That pain binds us
The we all share pain
Struggle to breath
I wish I can tell you this wasn't true

Life is breath
And breath is life
That is was the prophet said to me

One day breath comes easily
And another it is hard and burdened by its own weight.

There is an anointment in our sicknesses.
This is my Gospel to you
I cannot promise that it will ever be easy
But I can make it easier for you
Take my burdens.
Know my woes.
I will give you a yoke
That is easier than life.

Can you find these words
In the matter of your prophet
Can we agree
Life has its travesties
Each a death
Can you find
Its life?

++++++

I remember the day I met you
As if it were yesterday
You met me
Where I was waiting

There was no hesitation
I must have felt your heat
By the walk of your feet
Sending mine into a different vibration

To think that you
Smarter than me, gentler, more compassionate, and thoughtful
Could possibly love the sink hole that is me.

Your love remains.
Not just when you leave for work in the morning.
Your love of knowing I am, and all your loved ones are safe.
Right where you left them.

Sometimes I scare you.
I just want to explore more ways of how I can get people to love.
And experience the love of God
For the first time.
Every time.

You keep walking toward me.
No matter how high up I go.
Picking me up as I fall down.
Carrying me along the way.
A matrimony of you and me
But it's just your love of me
I hope I make you happy
More than I make you sad

I pray that the good
Far outweighs the bad

I know we are in this together
Because I could never do this alone
There is a oneness
In being owned.

+++++++

We are all called to holy orders.

A commandment to yourself
To be true to your destiny
To help others with what you have
Your original instructions
Given to you by Father Sky-Mother Earth
You are their child
The flower from the seed they planted.

We have been told

We have seen Their face
Every time we close our eyes
We see God's eyes
Staring back at us
The most focal point of you
And the most focal point of me
Are meeting each other
To fulfill our purpose
In each other's story
Who do you need me to be
And how can I help you with my resources
Given to me
By the Holy power
Are the holy orders
We give to one another.

Can we agree
To treat each other better
With the respect of self
With the hope of tomorrow
For us now
And generations to come

Forgive one another
For the wrong that we have done
In each other's minds
And in our hearts
For the known and unknown
And every idle word that comes out.

We if we helped one another
Along our ways
We will help ourselves
In the long run.

To one
With one
In one

Another.

* * *

**Joshua David Murphy (Esqueda) (they/he/she)** identifies as an indigenous-American who is also two-spirited and hard-of-hearing. They are the collective leader of the every, an inclusive spiritual community. In their free time, they enjoy practicing mediation and ballet as well as the sacred art of animal communication. He resides with his husband James, dog Theodore Grahams and cat Chihiro Louise Murphy in the wharf of Washington, D.C. Feel free to connect with them at theevery.squarespace.com and @t.h.e.e.v.e.r.y on all social media platforms.

## Love vs. Mr. Society

**Mary Ovie**

**(she/they)**

Man, a mistake spoken into existence. Was loved, but we are oblivious of what love truly is.
I was young, bright, beautiful. A few broken pieces here and there but forever vibrant, forever colorful. A child who has no clue about what and who they truly are but in their eyes are dreams.

A lover of the Lord who doesn't quite understand or concur with the word, but reference God still. They worked in the vineyard with their voice for the Lord tirelessly.

I was a soft skin Child with the evening glow on My 'Fro. I lived my life with so much passion and vigor, until You came into the picture.

Mr. Society.

A little older now, everything's not as it was
before. The doubts I had when I was younger took root. My affection;
"upside down," wrong, somehow, when I realized my heart stutters and drums when I'm around this pretty girl in school.

But I still love
God, or at least I try to.

Nobody warned me about you
"Mr. Society." Lest, I would have waited for you, prepared. I am now pieces of myself now. You came around and shattered me into a million tiny pieces with your hate.
Grinded me down with your words. You
told me I was the instruments of the last days.

Loud Whispers of how I was broken and needed to be fixed jerked me up at nights.
But how could I put so many tiny pieces back together, like collecting stardust drifting in space hoping it might become whole again? So
I tried praying my "illness" away from the deepest parts of my heart and in soft quiet prayers,
As if someone else would put my tiny little pieces together again.

I didn't want to be glared at like Mr. Society said people would.
I kept on praying but the more I did, the closer I spiraled into becoming something you said would destroy me. As I spiraled toward the void,
the more I felt at home with the idea of kissing my girl crush.
The more my strange love grew. The more disrupted and helpless I felt.

It's been two years now, I am
not who I was yesterday.

I have a better understanding,
now

I do not feel helpless anymore

I am
not Ill,

I am
not sick,

I am
not confused. This is
who I truly am. I am
whole and I am so precious in His sight still;

I've not thoroughly healed from your words,
Mr. Society.

The path to healing is slow, tiring and rocky.

I've not been able to step into the church of the lord since.

But I am trying my best to love myself and God.

I am surrounded by people who are like me, but stronger in faith.
I know that I am not alone.
I have met and seen God in the most unlikely places, and I realize
I am not who you say I am.

I am a soldier for Christ.

I am exactly just like Him.

I am not a sin.

I am not wrong.

I am me, and my strange love is not wrong.

---

*Thenotgoodenoughpoet.*

---

*Thenotgoodenoughpoet.*

* * *

**Mary Ovie** (she/they) is a young Nigerian Queer writer who writes to feel the large void in their heart. She lives in the peaceful but drama-filled city of Ogun state, Nigeria. She's currently preparing for their WASSCE exams. Her work _After_ was featured in a friend's Anthology DEPRESSION, thus making this their second published work.

**Selections**
**Simran Uppal**
**(they/them)**

## Nanak and Sharaf

Once Guru Nanak visited a saint
and said to them,
'Brother
why do you dress as a bride?
Saints love the Lord so they call us His "wives"
but He doesn't want nose rings or kohl round our eyes.'

The saint standing swept their sari to the side
hitched gold brocade with dark hands to their thigh, and
the glittering ripples of their heavy bridal dress,

red like red-gold mango flesh
red like bimba fruit and vermilion bindis,
brown henna dark and shimmering like a chestnut just born
splashed out in the shade of the gate-house.

Sharaf laughed and sang to Nanak:
'Yesterday this soul had an old woman's body;
tomorrow it's reborn somewhere else.

Our souls are bits of my Lover at play
and He skips between bodies like children with games.

Today He's a woman, then a man, or both,
a kothi, or hijra, aravani, kinnar.

The Lord dances in this body as He likes:
who am I to stop it
when His chin wants a beard
and His shoulders want a red-gold sari?'

## Garlands of my breath

After the great medieval female Sufi/Hindu, Mirabai, as famously sung by Nusrat Fateh Ali Khan as sanson ki mala pe.

Breaths rolling over my lips like
the beads of a rosary,
garlands of prayers twisting over fingers,
I remember my Lover's Name.

Lover! Be in front of my eyes,
    be held safe in my heart.
    I cannot see anyone else
    and I wish you were as blind.

Don't leave my arms before
love for you leaves my heart.
    The town where you live is more
    beautiful than the blue of the sky.

Breaths rolling over my lips like
the beads of a rosary,
garlands of prayers twisting over fingers,
I remember my Lover's Name.

    This is my praise!
    These are my prayers!

A lover adores one Lover in the temple,
another adores Another in the mosque.
But love drowns me so deeply in color
that the second and the first are the same.

When Radha met Krishna
love turned their senses into one and

Krishna was Radha and
Radha became Krishna.
Singing Your name on a lover's prayer-beads,
Krishna, singing, you become me.

There's no point in any of our work,
except thinking of love for our Lovers.

Breaths rolling over my lips like
the beads of a rosary,
garlands of prayers twisting over fingers,
I remember my Lover's Name.

## The Buddha turned my ex into a tangerine

If you peel a tangerine with so much love
you feel every spray of oil on your thumb,
bite on one piece, crumple
the skin of the segment and disappear it,
feel the flesh crackle into juice
and gush out between your molars
like tiny dams overflowing—
then that tangerine-moment fills your mind
so intimately that you and it aren't separate,
and you are completely alive.
Thich Nhat Hanh calls it tangerine meditation.

There were flowers on a bush near my house
even in December. He'd broken up with me two weeks
before then and the dampness made my jumpers heavy.
I took three deep breaths from one of the roses every day
because it was like eating a tangerine:
in those seconds I am the bit of the petal
that gives off the smell,
and my sadness is lighter, and delicious.

* * *

**Simran Uppal (they/them)** is a nonbinary British Punjabi poet, yoga teacher, and community organizer based in London, UK. After growing up at the edges of the UK's Punjabi Sikh community, they studied Classics at the University of Oxford, where they founded Coriander Theater, the UK's first theater company made up entirely of queer people of color. Simran is a three-time Barbican Young Poet, won a residency at the North Wall Arts Center, Oxford, and has worked with theatres in London, Berlin, and Mumbai. In their writing, they're interested in translation from medieval South Asian devotional poetry, particularly where it is erotic and ecstatic, as well as in queer British Asian lives, and the sacredness of cruising. Simran's poetry, lyric essays, and journalism on their grassroots politics and community building work have been published in The Independent, Burnt Roti, and in a major art book funded by the Consulate General of Italy; performances include a range of British queer collectives, English Heritage, The Isis, and most recently at the Barbican Concert Hall, Europe's largest arts center. Simran has also worked closely crafting movement and meditation practices with London's only queer youth center and helped set up the UK's first trade union for yoga teachers.

## A Collection of Feminist/Lesbian Christmas Carols
## Pastor Lucia Chappelle
**(she/her)**

### *O Come, All My Sisters*
***(O Come, All Ye Faithful)***

O come, all my sisters, joyful and collective,
Take pride in the new life that God lives in us!
Christ's new born Body, now in us appearing.

Refrain: Be open to the coming,
Be open to the coming,
Be open to the coming,
Of God in the flesh!

Sharing our crises, pooling our resources,
We're blest in an atmosphere of Sisterhood;
Nothing comes easy, everything is magic.

Refrain

God is our anchor, Christ our Predecessor,
Church makes us realize the glorious news:
Life is a love-gift, living is a gamble!

Refrain

## ***Indigent Sister***
### ***(Away in a Manger)***

Outside on a park bench, no place for a bed,
A poor starving sister lays down her gray head.
The chill of the night air, the city's heart cold,
While to Baby Jesus they offer their gold.

The shoppers are bustling, the Christmas lights blink,
Gift-giving is loving, or so some folks think;
But what must it look like to one such as she,
The indigent sister in her misery.

The love of the Christ child is not so abstract
To let me walk past you without looking back;
Stay with me, dear sister, and try to forgive
'Til the calling of Christmas is one I can live.

## *Feel Creation Grow More Whole*
### *(Hark! The Herald Angels Sing)*

Feel creation grow more whole
Glory to the mended soul!
This the reason Christ was sent—
Seal the human element.
Hierarchy isn't best
Put God's motives to the test:
Living life is not a curse—
Vengeful sacrifice is worse!

Refrain: Feel creation grow more whole
Glory to the mended soul!

We, the Church, experience
God's astounding imminence
Passed between each woman here
Bringing out the vision clear:
Forging our own Wanderground
Where our power can be found,
Where, like Christ, we unify
Flesh and spirit, nat'rally.

Refrain

I, like Christ, am one with God
I am healed through sisterlove,
Blessed fruit of my own womb,
Holy Amazon become!
Give and take my sisters' aid,
Both the midwife and the babe,
Woman and divine am I,
Limitless possibilities!

Refrain

## *What Faith Is This?*
### *(What Child Is This?)*

What faith is this that births the Word,
That braves the challenge of prophecy?
That risks the toll to yield control,
To rest on the truth of life's myst'ry?

Refrain: This, this is woman's faith,
To trust the magic that God creates.
Look, look to the wondrous sign,
The ebb and flow of the seasons.

What faith is this that turns the earth
From death to life in succession?
That sees God's face in Nature's pace:
The sun's return is salvation.

Refrain

## *Joy to the World!*
### *(Joy to the World!)*

Joy to the world! God's people come
To be Christ's hands and feet!
With open hearts and open minds
We seek to spread the peace…!

Joy to the earth! our sacred home,
Entrusted to our care!
By choosing to be human, God joined in our communion
All creatures everywhere…!

No more shall hate divide the saints,
Nor bigotry belong!
The gay, the bi, straight and intersex, the lesbians and transfolk
Join in the heav'nly song…!

God sent the Son to liberate
The Christ in each of us,
That greater things than Jesus did we would do also,
Work wonders with God's love…!

## *The Baby with the Two-Edged Sword*
### *(O Little Town of Bethlehem)*

The baby with the two-edged sword
Is in our midst today,
Seductive in her innocence
As at my breast she lay;
Yet see her dark eyes gleaning
The secrets of my soul,
The wall I built around myself
As loving takes its toll.

For Christ was born of Mary
And saw how it could be,
To lose that trusting openness
And vulnerability;
But could Christ have imagined
That love could be replaced,
By pious songs and spending throngs,
Much easier to face?

The pictures of the glowing child
Too holy to be hurt
Don't speak to the experience
Of treachery on earth;
But this new Christmas infant,
With wisdom in her smile,
Reminds us of love's double-edge—
To heal or to beguile.

Oh, baby with the two-edged sword
Cut through my frightened shield,
Inspire me with courage
For it's dangerous to feel.
Projection of my passion,
I take you back again;
Revive in me the faith to be
A gentle, risking friend!

## *Healing Night, Raging Night*
### *(Silent Night, Holy Night)*

Healing night, raging night
Women weep at their plight,
Circling nurturers comfort give,
Blessed with new kinds of spiritual gifts.
Christ's new body is born, Christ's new body is born!

Healing night, raging night,
Ne'er before such a sight,
Christian lesbians hand in hand,
Many theories, one mighty band,
Christ's new body is born, Christ's new body is born!

* * *

**Pastor Lucia Chappelle (she/her)** is the Social Justice Minister of Founders Metropolitan Community Church (MCC)/Iglesia de la Comunidad Metropolitana (ICM) Fundadora, Los Angeles. She was licensed clergy in MCC from 1977-1987, leading several congregations, serving as Dean of Samaritan Theological Institute, and representing the church in many social justice actions. She's currently a member of the Creative Worship Team, the Women's Spirituality Group, Azania: People of African Descent, the Deaf Ministry and the Archives Committee.

In her parallel career as a journalist in alternative media, Pastor Lucia helped start the LGBTQ radio show "IMRU" on KPFK-Pacifica Radio, Los Angeles in 1975, where she was Program Director from 1987-1994. She has been Associate Producer of the syndicated show T*his Way Out: The International LGBT Radio Magazine* since its inception in 1988. Working in print media as well as radio, she was the *WomanTimes* editor of the national LGBTQ newspaper *Coast to Coast Times* from 1977-1978.

Now a worldwide denomination, MCC was born in the LGBTQ community in October, 1968—nine months before the Stonewall Rebellion. During the late 1980s, another "rebellion" took place within MCC. A number of congregations arose with a specific mission to speak the Gospel to the lesbian feminist community. Lucia served as pastor of one of those congregations, DeColores MCC in Los Angeles, and wrote innovative worship materials. Her special gift was to re-write familiar Christian hymns with lesbian feminist images and language.

# TESTIMONIES
# &
# SERMONS

## An Aro/ace approach to adam before their encounter with the AnOther

**By Sulkiro Song**
**(she/they)**

Once upon my time before gender, before adults and older children began to correct me in the ways that I should be—what colors I should like, what toys I should play with, how to sit, why I should cover up in the presence of men, which characters I'm supposed to identify with, why I should pee sitting down, what future I should aspire for—I was adam in my own way, a one of a kind earth creature made in the image of god. Like the lone child of god in the garden, I was my parents' only child, roaming naked and free-range in the many apartments we lived in, each with thick layers of newspapers spread out for me to pee on.

In those days when my parents would retell and re-read the creation story to me, I found myself relating with adam for most of it. My favorite part was adam living in a lush, verdant garden with other animal friends and being in the presence of god as god's singular creature made in their likeness. It upset me that god would assume adam's loneliness without discussion and consent—that god would surgically remove a part of adam's body while adam lay unconscious to create another being. People had often assumed me to be lonely and would tell me that I should ask my parents to bear another sibling. I always felt threatened by such an idea—of having another being akin to me, so like me yet so distinct from me, ripping into my space with their presence, body, thoughts, and will. In such instances, I surprised people who knew me to be a quiet child by speaking out against such a horrible idea.

Although I liked to see myself as the incarnation of adam, I was apparently relating with the wrong character based on how I was supposed to pee. And I was peeing all wrong, too, or so I was told by people who did not live with me. Because I was so averse to fabrics confining my body and I'd throw off the clothes, diapers, and underwear that my mother tried to put on me, my mother quickly gave up running after me to re-wrap me in underwear and diapers. She paper trained me instead so that in my own time, I could run over to the thick bed of newspapers laid out on the floor in the middle of the living room, spread my legs out, and pee. Visitors coming over to our house would chide me and tell me that I was peeing all wrong—that I needed to learn how to pee sitting down. People then began to tell me that those who pee standing up relate with adam, and those who pee sitting down should relate with Eve. But since my parents did not reinforce these lessons to me growing up, I felt free in my nascent adamness, feeling the wind of god on my naked body in the cool of the day. Those were the days before gender.

The introduction of gender, sexuality, sex, church, and intimate relationships were like the sudden and jarring encounter with Eve—intrusive, shocking, overwhelming, horrid, disquieting, mystifying, and sublime.

When we immigrated to the U.S. from Korea, I had to reorient the way I related with myself and others in new ways. While the Korean language is generally free of gender-specific pronouns, and one could get away with just saying a series of verbs in sentences, English requires that a name, noun, or a gendered pronoun be spoken or written in nearly every sentence. English introduced gendered pronouns; in almost every sentence written and spoken, one has to state a name or pronoun to specify who was doing what. I had to be more cognizant of sex and gender binaries in English, whereas in Korean, I had to be more cognizant of birth order and social hierarchy in both speech and writing.

The concept of femininity and masculinity was also different in the U.S., and I found that they continued to shift in subtle ways as I moved through different regions. And just as the people in Korea had firm ideas of how those designated by society as sitting-down-urinaters should act, behave, desire, and live, many people in the U.S., especially those within church communities, had unyielding ideas as well.

Many of the church communities told the story of Adam & Eve in ways that I could no longer relate to—as morality lessons evidencing a divinely prescribed sex binary and gender binary, the primacy of heterosexuality, the fallenness of humankind, and the special weakness and evil of women.

People also reinterpreted my identity through the filter of patriarchal white supremacist orientalism that drew from imperialist military sexual violence against girls and women. For a while, even well into my adulthood, I was The Asian Girl. Sometimes, The Hot Asian Girl. These were descriptions that I could not relate with, but again, just as adults and older children in my toddlerhood tried to inculcate into me how I should exist, people, particularly men, tried to tell me what I was. Those who "love Asian culture" projected onto me their desires of a possible Asian anime girlfriend. It did not matter that I had come out multiple times to people as asexual. My asexuality was usually quickly forgotten, dismissed, or taken up as a challenge. They did not see me in the likeness of god, but an object of imperial conquest. It did not matter if I could not reciprocate romantic or sexual attraction. For men, especially white men in the U.S., femininity and heterosexuality were assumed onto me without discussion and without consent.

Being an open-minded pan aro/ace, I had been in a couple of intense partnerships that involved long, dialectic explorations of our identities and the universe. Some of the fights were just as intense, and it was in those moments that felt frustratingly overwhelming—to stare across space into a person whose mind I could not penetrate. To realize that there can be no amount of words that could truly be a bridge to that very other mind which at many times felt like a completely separate and foreign universe separated by an infinite chasm from the universe of my own being. And I imagine that is how adam must have felt sometimes when adam stared back at Eve in moments of altercation or in moments of admiration. Perhaps adam wondered, "how could this person who is so like me be so utterly far from what I am?" I imagine moments of excitement when adam felt that they were connecting with Eve, projecting onto her their own thoughts and desires, only to be shattered by the realization later that Eve is her very own person despite having been made from adam's side.

I realize that I am doing the very same thing—projecting—onto your Adam & Eve. To me, they are genderless and still new and ignorant in the possibilities of their many expressions including sexuality. Just as I was perplexed by why people assumed me to be heterosexual, I did not know why it had to be that adam and Eve are heterosexual. How would Adam and Eve even know of their sexualities? The story seems to imply that they lived together isolated from other societies. So how would they even know if they had not encountered others to figure out their attractions and desires?

In seminary, I learned that there were medieval rabbis who believed adam to be intersex or androgynous due to the Hebrew wordings regarding adam in Genesis 1:27. And so I was determined that my adam and Eve are like me, made in my image, as I am made in the image of god.

There were many nights after long shifts of working and socializing that I would go up to the mountain for lone night hikes. These night hikes were my outlets to withdraw from the cacophony of information, connections, and projections, and draw near to god, whom I felt truly connected with when I would pray/ramble/converse in Korean. In the cool of the night under the faint Milky Way, I'd imagine myself to be adam—just a child, just a lone child without the burden of having to explain myself to anyone, without the traumatic encounter with AnOther, before gender, before sex and sexuality, and before the betrayal of divine assumption.

* * *

**송 슬기로 Sulkiro Song (she/they)** holds a Master in Divinity in biblical studies from Union Theological Seminary and holds special interests in fine loose-leaf teas, queer BIPOC expressions of Satanism, and the unification of the severed Koreas.

## Learning to Delight in My Queerness
**Naiomi Gonzalez**
**(she/they)**

Growing up, I was taught to hate my queerness. I was told I was an "abomination" to God, that my queerness was offensive to God. In order to love God, I needed to make a choice: my faith, or my queerness. I spent many nights in anguish, praying to God to make me the perfect, straight, submissive cisgender woman.

I spent most of my days pretending *to be* that perfect woman: I wore knee-length skirts; I kept my messy and tangled hair long; I prepared myself for marriage to a straight man by trying be less opinionated and loud; I read the Bible and prayed every day; and I attended services multiple times a week. And yet, I often felt like a fraud. "God knows the heart of every person," my pastor frequently preached. Which meant God knew that I was faking it.

My faith was slowly killing me—exacerbating my mental illness and leaving mental and physical scars on my body. Finally, I decided I had to leave my faith or else I would allow myself to be so overcome with despair that I would die. But leaving Christianity and God behind pained my soul. My love for God was real. God was the reason I got up in the morning. My faith wasn't just a phase, but a core part of my identity, and to leave that part of me behind felt like abandoning a key part of my soul.

After leaving my childhood church, I frequently asked myself and my peers, "could I be Christian and Queer?" The answer I often received both from Christians and from my Queer peers was "absolutely not." I had to choose one or the other. But how could I choose between the faith that gave my life meaning and purpose and my queerness? I was told by so many people that my queerness was a barrier to my faith and my faith was a barrier to living an authentic life.

In a desperate bid to save my faith, I attended seminary. There, I met queer professors, students, pastors and future pastors who showed me that faith and queerness can coexist. Their lives proved that my faith and my queerness could illuminate each other. There was the dean of students at the seminary, who was ordained and openly spoke about her relationship with another woman. My transgender peers challenged my patriarchal notions of God. Who was I to say that God was only "male?" Who was I to limit God?

Seminary taught me to embrace all aspects of my humanity. My peers and professors assured me I didn't have to choose between my faith and my queerness. I could both love God and love myself in all of my queer, nonbinary glory. In fact, they showed me that God didn't just accept me, but God delighted in me.

My queerness wasn't a curse sent to me by Satan to dissuade me from following God, but rather my queerness was a gift from God. My queerness allows me to experience God in ways that cis-gender, straight people find difficult. My being nonbinary is a reflection of a God who transcends gender identity. God is male, female, neither, and everything in between. My queerness is an expression of God's expansive love, a love that doesn't discriminate based on race, gender expression, or sexual orientation.

My intersectional identities—queer, nonbinary, and Latinx—also allow me to experience in very tangible ways the God of the marginalized. I experience on a daily basis, the God who became human not to rescue humanity from eternal torment but to usher in a world where violence, oppression, and hatred are no more. The God who sides with the oppressed or marginalized became human—became one of the oppressed and marginalized. God became one of us. My queerness doesn't separate me from God, but rather, it brings me closer to God.

* * *

**Naiomi Gonzalez (she/they)** identifies as a Queer, nonbinary, Latinx Christian. They have an M.Div from Brite Divinity School, an MA in Islamic and Middle Eastern Studies from George Mason University and an MA in History at Texas Christian University. They have a variety of interests, but they are particularly passionate about exploring the ways in which Christianity has been, and continues to be, historically used to both justify and resist state violence, racism, and injustice. Her blog can be found at faithfullyradicalchristian.wordpress.com @faithfullyradicalchristian on IG

## Lamentations of a Salt Flat

**Kōan Anne Brink**
**(they/them)**

My partner and I have established a recent ritual of listening to public radio sermons on long drives. The transmissions are often poor, the white noise of static cutting and overlaying the sermon with classical piano or country music, or, in some instances, an advertisement for a long-distance rifle range. In this particular sermon there is what appears to be a sort of oral treatise on thirst. The preacher today is speaking of God's love in metaphors of milk. Human beings are babies who lament the milk of God's love. Now this is all I can see across the mountains. R is not clothed in a white T-shirt, but in a thin layer of cotton milk as he drives East. The valleys are not filled with the reflections of cloud shadows, but with the reflections of milk in the grass.

* * *

Soon, the salt flats will begin to appear outside the window too, clinging to the corners of shallow rock like dried sleep in the eyes. The word "lament" comes from the Latin *lamenta,* meaning to "weep" or "wail." As in: A vast salt flat in the Western landscape *laments* their former body as a prehistoric lake. The lake can take the shape of a song or a piece of music, or a poem expressing sorrow. It often mourns (a person's loss or death). Because of the evaporating lake levels, what is classified as an island or a peninsula on a map year-to-year shifts. In other words, the perception of impermanent bodies in space shifts.

* * *

The flats perfectly reflect the mountains around them, creating jagged, milky moths in their wake. The mirage of water on their surface appears more like water than actual water. When did the idea of water become its most accurate definition? When did the idea of a body become the most accurate definition of a body, or of the passing of time? To take the entirety of the landscape in is to be driving towards a perpetually moving lake that recedes on the horizon.

* * *

I want to say something affirming here about being nonbinary in my gender expression, and how this identity has formed a space to be freer as a body on Earth, how the impermanence of this very space might bring me closer to something like God. Although I think the word "free" is very dangerous, and lately, what I have been feeling are immense griefs, the plurality of griefs well in my lungs on the highway, until they pour into a song of uncontrollable crying. I view these sensations as a process of moving towards wholeness, of feeling sharp edges an acceptance that the emptiness (fullness) I seek is only a practice of opening to a vast number of holes over and over again. Eventually, I will open to so many holes they will fit together, creating more oxygen for my lungs. I cannot get rid of this child crying inside of me, but I can wake them up. Waking them up from the salt sleep will occur inside the simultaneous holes; it will never occur in actualizing an idea of wholeness.

* * *

In looking out the window, I think I am not reaching out to God so much as a void, which feels like a kind of unconditional love in its possibility of fullness, like the repetition of *no's* strung throughout the Heart Sūtra, a bloodline across time and space—*no eyes, no ears, no nose, no tongue, no body*—Where the *no's* create holes are pools of dried salt in the valley; their negations cry out to thirst, to the formation of a life on earth.

* * *

I thought all small-town motels still had Bibles tucked into their nightstand drawers; this particular one does not. Luckily, I have two stashed away in the truck. One is left over from divinity school, the other belonged to my late grandmother. I sit inside the motel's cocktail lounge along Route 50, which *Life Magazine* called, in 1966, "the loneliest route in America." The Book of Lamentations, open on the table before me, begins: "How lonely sits the city." I stab a Maraschino cherry with the tip of my straw. The basis of this book is a touchstone lamentation. The city, personified as a woman, is wailing out to God for her newfound emptiness. The poem operates as a kind of funeral dirge for all who have been lost within its walls. It gathers them in the acrostic lines of its fingers.

* * *

Sometimes I laugh and catch myself sounding like my grandmother, but it's too late to stop, so I keep laughing. That is a form of mourning, that laughter also a kind of lament. There are all kinds of laments around us we don't automatically classify as mourning. The pushing of an empty shopping cart through a supermarket, for example. The way the sound of laughter connects us in time to someone who has passed. I think a lament does not necessarily "sound" like our habitual idea of sadness, or water, or salt. For a thing to be truly heartbreaking, it is often removed from the boundary of being clearly identifiable as a static break; it turns instead into a form of dailiness, a slow thirst over time. The holding of a heavy iron teapot is a lament in its desire for boiled water.

Digging a hole in the garden and planting flowers, the future necks dream of water. The thirstiest things on earth we might never even notice.

* * *

**Kōan Anne Brink (they/them)** was born and raised in Minnesota. They are the author of the poetry chapbook *The End of Lake Superior* (Above/Ground, 2021). Kōan currently holds the position of Art Writing Fellow at The Cooper Union. Raised Lutheran, they are also a lay ordained Sōtō Zen student practicing with teachers at Brooklyn Zen Center, where they are an active member in the LGBTQ Dharma Share. Their current home is Austin, Texas.

## When Queer Meets Christ
## Kaweme Mambwe
### (she/her)

Growing up as a gay transgender woman in an utterly homophobic and transphobic society has proved to be a great challenge. There comes a time in the life of nearly every LGBTQIAS2+ identifying Christian where they begin to question their faith, are deemed as deviants by other straight Christians, and slowly stray away from the Christian path. I am but an example of the said experience and I would like to share it with you.

Coming out to someone in my country would mean being shunned by every member of the community and worse still, would warrant one 14 years to life imprisonment. As if that is not enough, organizations working against queer people have been established and their job is to sow the seed of homophobia. LGBTQIAS2+ people are hated by almost everyone where I live—even those who would be considered the most violent are seen to be better than a queer-identifying person.

I was raised in an Adventist household that is extremely conservative and homophobic. My family and I would go to church every Saturday morning and leave in the late evening. There was nothing I loved more than singing praises for the lord and worshipping him. I was actively engaged in programs at my church that involved using one's talents to glorify the lord. Soon enough, I was baptized but little did I know that the worst was yet to come.

My attitude towards Church slowly began to grow negative when I began to notice the high level of hypocrisy among my fellow straight congregants. Most of the congregants preached what they did not do. One Saturday afternoon, during church service the pastor preached about how homosexuals and "gender-deviants" would rot in hell simply because of their nature. I was seething with rage when I heard that but I dared not show it. I had my last straw.

I decided not to set foot in my church or any other church for good. Soon enough, I felt like God didn't love me and that I was as useful as a chocolate teapot in his house. I stopped praying and reading the Bible altogether, and out of rage, I began to go against Christianity in every way.

After months of hating Christianity and building a wall around my heart to keep out God, I began to feel empty inside and contemplating suicide became something I entertained daily. I began to self-hurt myself physically by cutting myself whenever I felt like it.

One night, I felt so helpless that I decided to pray. I was tired of hurting inside and feeling helpless. I knelt down beside my bed and prayed. No sooner had I finished praying than I felt God's love with me. At that moment I knew God loved me regardless of my sexual orientation and gender identity. Finding online communities of like-minded individuals has been a great blessing indeed.

My faith is now largely shaped by developing a loving relationship with God and seeing him as my loving savior, lord, and friend. I believe God is love and to love someone past their flaws is truly Christ-like. Lastly, if you are part of the LGBTQIAS2+ community, God loves you just as much as he loves your straight counterparts.

* * *

**Kaweme Mambwe (she/her)** is a teenage author. She identifies as a gay transgender woman, with pronouns she/her. She is a Christian by faith and believes in love and inclusion for all regardless of our differences. As an author, she goes by the pseudonym; Kreamy Christian. She is an aspiring medical doctor. In her free time she loves practicing belly dancing of all forms, singing, and thinking of new ideas for my novel writing. She loves supporting the queer community however she can, building new friendships, and learning about different cultures and customs.

## A Communion of Gender Euphoria

**Eric Busby**
**(they/him)**

*Southern Charm and Debutante Hate-Worship*

For the purposes of this paper, I will call her K. She and I were friendly in the small Alabama brick sidewalk town where I studied for my undergraduate degree and I jumped at the chance to attend spring formal with her. After all, she was a modern-day Southern belle—in a top sorority, walked in Cotillion, drank Bud Lite at 18, complained about trashy girls in the freshman class while smoking a Marlboro—she was a cool-girl-deb (short for debutante), a noteworthy class in the Southern caste system as defined (by me for me) below:

***Cool-Girl-Deb (n.): a female identifying young 20-something who exists and maintains her place at the top of the Southeastern U.S. ecosystem by balancing "it-girl" appropriation and Southern societal expectations. Identifiers include but are not limited to: (1) being more liberal than daddy but remaining silent on Bernie, (2) skipping church, sorority chapter (she can afford the fine) but making it to family supper on Sunday, (3) bemoaning social conformity with a designer baguette in the right hand and a vape pen in the left, (4) moving to Nashville, Atlanta or Austin in three years and becoming a lady-who-lunches in 15.***

It's no surprise this archetype of Southern Camp is a total queer icon. (Every lady's group in Birmingham has at least one gay, usually a decorator that they pass around.) It is my opinion, with a healthy dose of experience, that queer folk, specifically homosexual cis or cis-passing men like myself, have an entangling experience with these women. It looks like love but stings like hate—they have something you're close to having, but it is always an arm's length away.

*Drag: Summer Humidity and Sexuality*

Last year I attended my first drag show on Church Street in the July heat of downtown Nashville. Deception was the name of one of the night's hostesses. She wore a picture perfect golden blonde, shoulder length 'do with curled tips and a long pageant dress. Her teeth are white and her mascara is immaculate—not too little, not too much, just like a granny and Jesus would want. She had turned herself into the perfect Southern belle—an act that I had secretly (or not so secretly) always tried to access. Where were my white gloves? If I had shiny hair and a tiny waist, would that not earn me space to be on parade for the town? This silent but quietly devastating delineation between me and the girls I grew up around—this tension between affection and jealousy—was pronounced in Deception's performance as she joked about her virginal dignity and Southern airs and graces.

I saw someone carving space between affection and jealousy. To imitate is flattery, but is the imitation out of hatred or admiration? Or neither? Fast forward eight months, a move to New York, and one semester of seminary later and I find myself speaking with James, a Union graduate themself who is a drag performer and artist, even leading "drag chapels" in which a liturgy is served with a queering twist. When asked about the masculine/feminine binary articulated in drag and from where the powerful experience of drag emanates its strength, their response was situated on the ability to access, rather than feminine power over masculinity or a manipulation of masculinity, the elusive feeling of gender euphoria (GE). I started this paper expecting to write about drag and stumbled into GE—a new world that is mostly unmapped but expansive and abundant. This makes perfect sense. Of course, the power is not in Deception's recreation of her wealthy Sunday school teacher, but in her ability to create a gender fluid atmosphere that is freeing for those inhabiting the space. Note to self: find out more.

*Machetes against Rainbow Brick*

It became quickly apparent that research into Gender Euphoria would not come easily. The terrain is still wild and untamed and one really needs a sharpened machete to cut through the weeds to take each next step. To begin, I opened Homosaurus.org, an international database developed in 1997 in response to institutional misuse or misunderstanding of queer categorization in environments like library archives that may still be using outdated Subject Heading terminology from the U.S. Library of Congress. Homosaurus is noteworthy in that seven years ago, the Digital Transgender Archives became one of the first institutional archive collections to utilize Homosaurus' vocabulary as their primary Subject Headings for all archival data—a major step in democratizing access to gender queer resources (homosaurus.org, 2022). Homosaurus is thusly a monolithic destination for those searching out an understanding of queer lifestyles and languages. I was shocked to find that this database, which has hundreds of terms (from Coming Out to Breast Size, Tantric Sex to Micropenis) doesn't include Gender Euphoria in their list of terms relevant to queer lives (homosaurus.org, 2022.)

And so, the journey stretched outward, to find out what GE might truly be so that it may be accessed. One journal article from New Mexico University in 2021, "Imagining Gender Euphoria," one of the more helpful articles in the venture to traverse the concept of gender euphoria, gives a contradictory definition in its opening page. The author defines GE as "the conviction that gender diverse people are valid in (their) gender identities, regardless of standards of embodiment." Author Kai McKinney misses the mark in this from quite an elementary standpoint (McKinney, 2021, iii.). Euphoria, as defined by the Collins English Dictionary, is a "feeling of great elation." Elation is a far cry from conviction, defined in the same dictionary as "a fixed or firmly held belief "(dictionary.com, 2022). I concede that perhaps acts of conviction might make spaces for euphoric moments, and maybe even the other way round, but the two are not the same.

In an article from the Norwegian Agder University journal *Elsevier Masso*n, author E.E.P. Benestad in their piece titled "From Gender Dysphoria to Gender Euphoria" never actually uses the word 'euphoria' except in reference to the title of the piece. Benestad gives an implied definition in the article summary indicating that the goal of this gender-focused therapeutic work is synchronicity between a client's gendered self-perception and social perception, giving rise to "gender belonging" (Benestad, 2010, 225). While there is no concrete definition provided, there is resonance in the concept of gender belonging. However, I would argue that the dependence upon the other-ed perception of oneself is a barrier to true euphoria, which is an intrinsic state of well-being and release. We are so accustomed to the systematic structuring of information produced in the Enlightenment of the 18th and 19th centuries, that what is simply the educational system we were raised into, we, without thought, consider logic. This type of logic, which places ideas, concepts, and experiences into binary opposition to "counter" ideas, concepts, and experiences, is the causation of issues arising in definitions like the one described above where defining traits lean heavily on opposing ideals rather than lived experience.

I argue that binary thinking will always exclude queerness, which is innately absent in opposing enemy lines. To queer ethics, theology and institutions cannot simply add rainbow bricks with neon pink mortar to existing red clay structures. True queer understandings are outside of structured states, like the plane flying above or the groundwater meters beneath. In Enlightened thinking, queer ideas will not be found at eye level and so I say the truest definitions of Gender Euphoria that can be found at present lie in sources more closely related to humanity.

*Along Danced TikTok (and several other resources).*

She is chaos. She is frenzy. She is a 15 second hit of Dopamine.

She is TikTok. And she is quite powerful in deconstructing the ways in which the Enlightenment fucked over our ability to communally learn and share information. In a TikTok posted by @mx.deran on the 16th of January 2021, content creator Ty Deran describes gender euphoria in their bedroom by showing off themself wearing a new off-the-shoulder floral-patterned cream ruffle-topped high-low dress in Valentino Rockstud ankle strap pumps. (The real statement is the eyebrow and nose highlight, but I digress.) With shoulders back and cheeks bright with un-hesitated happiness, they define GE with more than just words but also through their body in the movement of their hands and their pauses to savor each breath, in and out. Ty concludes with, "I see myself and that is a gift. That is such a gift" (Deran, 2022.)

Similarly, in a section entitled "The Diva Gender Euphoria Survey," London-based magazine *Diva* gave responses to questions around transgender people's experiences of gender and self-actualization. In response to a question that would give definition to GE, respondents stated the following: GE is the feeling of "wearing my sister's green velvet skirt," "the sun after darkness," and "permission" (Diva, 2022). The enfleshed experience of gender euphoria is discovered in the way these self-identified characteristics are offered up by those abused at the hands of gender *dys*phoria. GE allows transgender people to *feel* their *own* body inside of their soul, rather than searching for themselves *without*-of themselves.

Plume is a new home-healthcare system developed for person's seeking gender affirming therapies that strives to alleviate the stressors commonly associated with seeking medical treatment inside a queer body such as fear of doctor's offices, fear of medically based micro-aggression, and fear of being misgendered (Plume.com, 2022). Further, most medical services rely on a Gender *DYS*phoria diagnosis before being able to prescribe gender-affirming treatments. To do so, is to rely on the language of the oppressor which systematically and innately refutes any acknowledgement of gender outside of the male/female binary. GD as a diagnosis implies that the struggle *towards* gender euphoria is merely a person struggling inside of themselves for physical congruence with soul-level traits while ignoring the struggles stemming from a pandemically heteronormative society (McKinney, 2021, p. 19). Plume offers new routes to care and new definitions of GE which, based on the lack of information at the academic level, are more embodied and more focused on the self-to-self model of understanding GE for which I am advocating. Plume's definition is below.

*"(1) Cognitive Euphoria: when a person's mind fully accepts and loves their gender identity, with feelings of "I love myself" and "I am lovable as my authentic self (2) Social Euphoria: when others gender the person correctly, title them correctly, and call them by the right name, it sparks a powerful sense of happiness and belonging; especially important with family members, coworkers, and friends because it creates community (3) Body Euphoria: An overall sense of comfort, ease, and enjoyment of the person's body, including feeling "right sized," in the right body, and free within this physical form"*

*Deception! Deception! Deception!*

When James, the former Union student and drag queen, described the feeling of drag as gender euphoric, I knew I had to investigate further. Topically, this proved to be as wide-open and multifaceted as the Pacific Ocean. GE isn't one thing, it is many—in the same way that people and our experiences are many. Academically, the research and historic data discovered make an important case regarding the deconstruction of the source of gender dysphoria as being something that is without, as opposed to within a trans, genderqueer or nonbinary person. These sources, however, lack in their ability to offer a true definition of what a world without dysphoria would look like. This is where the self-expressed sources like TikTok become such key figures. As gender is an enfleshed experience, so must the definition of GE represent and *guide towards* a life-affirming feeling of embodied euphoric power.

It is this embodied power that Deception offered to me on that humid night in Tennessee last year—the ability to step out of the binary locking me in an arm's length hate-worship of the girls I grew up loving. Gender Euphoria is an accessible power which allows binaries to evaporate, even momentarily, so that queer persons can feel themselves, and hopefully, this feeling of one's self leads to healing as one finds and accesses more of themself. In *Non-Binary Lives*, Reverend Rowan Bombadil describes spaces like this as being spaces where "the queer bodies in the room that are tense with trepidation, taut with that question-mark we carry around our own welcomeness every damn day, (can) relax a little and (be) loved as our shapeshifting, time-travelling, gender-fucking selves." They state that they find these spaces to be "medicine for our queer hearts, bodies and spirits" (Bombadil, 2020, 102-103). I am comfortable with the medical metaphor, but would, in the context of spiritual care, push one step further. When Deception offers up the space to feel welcomed inside of yourself *by yourself*, the space to feel gender euphoric, she is offering up communion—the ability to take one's own body as bread, good for feeding the soul, and one's own blood as forgiveness, good for redemption of wrong. Perhaps gender euphoria is the Eucharist rite for the queer saints—a ritual in which misplacement in an oppressively gendered system can be redeemed into the renewal and regeneration of life outside the binary.

* * *

*Bibliography:*

*Benestad, E. E. P. (2010). From Gender Dysphoria to Gender Euphoria: An Assisted Journey. Sexologies, 19(4), 225-231.*

*Bombaldi, R. (2020). Queer Identity as a Spiritual Calling. Non-Binary Lives: An Anthology of Intersecting Identities, 101-104*

*Deran, T. (2022, 01). @mx.deran: The Power of Gender Euphoria. https://vm.tiktok.com/ZTdUCbr4D/.*

*Homosaurus, (2022). Mission, History, & Vocabulary. https://homosaurus.org/*

*McKinney, K. W. (2021). Imagining gender euphoria: An alternative to culturally hegemonic understandings of transgender embodiment (Order No. 28777642). Available from ProQuest Dissertations & Theses Global, vii-84.*

*Noyce, E. (2022, 01). The DIVA gender euphoria survey. Diva, 28-31.*

*Plume Health Services. (2021, 09). What are Gender Dysphoria & Gender Euphoria. https://getplume.co/blog/what-are-gender-dysphoria-and-gender-euphoria/*

* * *

**Eric Busby (they/him)** is a first year Master of Divinity at Union Theological Seminary student in the City of New York concentrating in Theology and the Arts with a specific focus on queering charismatic faith practices and understandings. Formerly a social worker turned designer and stylist, Eric, a recovering Southern Baptist, hopes to use their specific educational training to bridge gaps between embodied creativity and theological knowledge.

## God Calls Me: To Ministry and to Transition
## King Julez
### (they/them)

God Calls Me: to Ministry and to Transition

I am transgender, I am nonbinary, I am queer, I am a holy child of God.

I am baptized, I am confirmed, I am on the candidacy pathway in The United Church of Canada; I am a holy child of God.

These two streams of my identity are inextricably linked because God planned it that way. It has taken me a long time to be comfortable combining these streams, and confidently announcing one in parallel with the other. Being visible in this way has brought me more joy than I can put into words. I feel closer to myself than I ever have, and closer to God than before I began transitioning. I am able to live my life as an experiment; always checking in with myself and the world to be sure what I'm doing is making me happy and being authentically true. I mean, if I'm out of the closet I might as well queer-up every moment possible.

Being visible also has caused me much loss. I've lost my mother, my father, my grandmother, and my uncle. The people who were closest to me abandoned me for the sole reason of my transness. I've lost job opportunities and I've had to change medical professionals more times than I can count simply because they do not know about transgender healthcare. There are obstacles and boundaries I face in relation to my transition every day; each new person I meet is another situation in which I need to come out and hope that there is understanding and respect. The human experience is full of pain and hardship—Jesus exemplified this—but these things are necessary for what is to come (unfortunately).

Most everything I know about love is through the church and I knew it as a child—the first trans people I ever met were in the church. The first lesbians I met were in church. The first gay man I met was leading the regional retreats I went to. I didn't meet a queer person outside of the church until I was around 16 or 17 years old—a true thank you to the churches I was a part of as a child for showing myself and other queer folks that your spaces were not only safe, but also places for us to lead. Queerness and queer love (for the self, or for another) paves such a way to understanding God or vice versa. I don't know if I knew of my queerness as a child but God surrounded me with people who would show me in the very place where I was learning what love was about. My transness and my queerness are inextricably linked to my faith and my call to ministry because God intended them to be. The losses I face are necessary for the human experience, but my transness is holy and meant to take up space in the church.

My being visible and out potentially paves way for others who aren't, cannot, don't know, or have yet to learn. I live my life out and visible in spite of how hard it is, or how many losses come from it. God has called me into transition the same as I am called into ministry. I discern my gender every day the same way I discern my call to ministry; I pray, I think, I reflect, I take in my surroundings, I listen for God's message. Transition is a holy and blessed experience that, for me, is never ending. I will always be in transition, that is my beauty in being nonbinary. I am constantly going to be moving from space to space finding what makes me the most comfortable in the most ambiguous sense of the word. With my ministry, I imagine I will move from space to space much in the same way: what is God's message and how can this community be the most comfortable place to hear that message? I bring my full and queer self to church (to the *front* of the church) to show that this is the church God wants.

My body is my church and God's message is my transition. Is transgressing boundaries not what God's love is all about?

I am baptized, I am confirmed, I am on the candidacy pathway in The United Church of Canada, I am a holy child of God.

I am transgender, I am nonbinary, I am queer, I am a holy child of God.

* * *

**King Julez (they/them)** is a trans nonbinary drag clown and a Master of Divinity student at Emmanuel College in Toronto, Ontario, Canada. They are pursuing a career in ordained ministry within The United Church of Canada as a drag clown. Presently, they are the chair of the board for Affirm United/ S'affirmer Ensemble—an organization that promotes full inclusion of queer folks in The United Church of Canada and beyond.

# Taste and See and Know
## Micah Brady
### (she/her)

I discovered my sexuality in a worship service. I often forget this detail, finding it insignificant.

It sprung upon me, matter-of-fact, like the knowledge had always hovered in a formless cloud in the back of my mind. It only took a moment of focus to determine its shape, to see a hidden resemblance of reality in its often ordinary and overlooked presence. I knew instinctively, not finding the answer within myself—rather, the fact was so true that it presented itself to me. I saw its striking hues and deep texture form tangibly before my eyes for the first time.

It only took a moment. The blue-green stage lights swirled over the congregants as the song ascended throughout the sanctuary, snapping my eyes simultaneously outward and inward: outward, toward the worship band and away from the girls in pews surrounding me; and inward, toward the clearing fog that had long shadowed my mental skyscape, revealing that I had, in fact, been staring at girls.

Disturbed, I peered over at some boys a few seats away. I suddenly knew that I found many people around me worthy of staring.

My father recently told me that all knowledge is a gift.

In eighth grade—the day of this worship service—I received a gift. I opened it with curiosity like a kid on Christmas morning, tearing away in anxious anticipation.

When I unfastened the gift, I saw myself: my body and her being, her knowledge and her desires. Surveying the contents within, I recognized the gift I held because I had witnessed other people receive it. I had never envied it; in fact, I had pitied recipients of this gift. Now I held it in my hands.

I thanked God kindly for the gift though I loathed it—in the same way you thank a distant relative before sliding the gift into the corner of your closet, waiting for an opportunity to discard it unnoticed.

I knew what the gift meant, and in the same moment I knew, I resolved; in the same moment it felt like angels had descended from the heavens to spell it out in clear skywriting, I resolved to look down from the heavens. I wouldn't look upward again for five years, ignoring the divinely bestowed sign.

On the ground, I wandered in dark pits of doubt, enveloped in a fog of my own narrow vision. The thick gray dulled my senses, hues losing color in the darkness and blurring to a haze. I could not feel texture, I could not see depth, I could not taste vibrant truth on my tongue. I could only tell black from white—which wasn't much at all.

I slowed, dragging myself and stumbling through the fog while my body existed far away, her preaching a soft echo. She spoke to me, "They who have ears, let them hear!" but without my body I had no ears. I could not hear; I could not taste and see.

But the church comforted me. "Better to have blind faith than to trust your sight," the church said. "Better to leave her behind than to follow her," the church said. "Better to lose your ears than to hear her false prophecy," the church said.

I did not trust my body. I had learned that she was the root of rebellion, her senses a slippery slope. Her desires tended toward temptation though the Spirit ached for salvation.

"For the desires of the flesh are against the Spirit, and the desires of the Spirit are against the flesh, for these are opposed to each other, to keep you from doing the things you want to" (Galatians 5:17, ESV).

I did not trust her to live in the world, to speak and act without my guidance or permission. I wanted more than to just leave her behind; I wanted to destroy her, rend her from existence. So, I dragged her, exhausted and hopeless as I was, crucified her and held her in the grave. In the gray ground I crushed her senseless, buried in the belief that the eternal death of my body was the price of spiritual resurrection.

But she was not silenced.

Five years later, she rose again. She reclaimed her voice and her sensations, so much so that she invaded my foggy slums, flipping tables and toppling my flimsy temple with her tumultuous preaching.

Her destruction complete, her knowledge demanding, she knelt down beside me in the wreckage of my stubborn refuge and gave me ears. Then she told me a story I knew but had never accepted.

She said we are a work of art, a symbiotic creation. Little did I know, my eighth-grade sexuality was my incarnation, God's physical gift to my spiritual formation. Born like a gift on Christmas day, the physical and spiritual united at God's declaration, thus constituting their separation a desecration. As Jesus' birth revealed our God, my body too became a revelation. She said listen to what she had to reveal. The desires of the flesh are against the Spirit, so our Lord not only resurrected his Spirit but his body too. He did not discard it nor did he leave it in the grave like I had tried to do.

So, on that day of my incarnation, my body began to grow, waiting patiently, speaking whispers and prophecies until she broke out into sermons, enduring time for the sake of crucifixion.

When the time came, she burst forth from the grave, powerful and purified by the blood of the cross, shouting praises on the ground stained with damnation. She said it is through her eyes and ears and hands that I know and receive God's gifts of creation. Our being is God's image in bodily manifestation, so we must together participate in divine sanctification.

As I exist, God reveals. As God reveals, I know; and because I know, I worship. I continually open the gift and live my thankfulness, partaking in the bodily sacrament that I may taste and see and know.

All knowledge is a gift, and perhaps God gives it through the continual resurrection of body and soul.

* * *

**Micah Brady (she/her)** is a demisexual, panromatic Christian living in Los Angeles. She is a recent English writing graduate of Biola University and strives to heal the separation of the LGBTQ+ community and the church with her words. In her free time, she loves reading, hiking, climbing, and she *occasionally* blogs at www.micahbradyportfolio.com

## Queerness as Sacred Practice
## By Carly Reiner
### (they/she)

I've come to learn that theology—or what we say we believe about god and whose spiritual history gets told—really, really matters. Our theology deeply impacts people's lives and toxic theology is real violence. While working as a school counselor, I had a nine-year-old come out to me, and the next words out of their mouth were, "but I know people say it is a sin." Already this theology was teaching her to associate something beautiful about herself with something evil; something somehow contrary to the divine. What is closer to the divine than expansive love? What else are god's plans other than abundant and radical love for ourselves and one another?

Though trans and queer people have existed as spiritual leaders throughout history and across cultures, the white cishetero patriarchy and colonialism have fought hard to erase these narratives.

After being rejected from my own Christian community for being queer, I began pursuing my Master of Divinity degree at Union Theological Seminary in search of answers to the question of how my queer identity and my Christian identity could be in communion with one another. I found that I was not alone in this endeavor. So many of us were looking to heal from our own spiritual trauma while learning how to carry out anti-racist, queer-centered ministries. So many people that I connected with were seeking out healing from dominant western theologies and systems that alienate us from our own bodies, teach us to fragment our identities, and mistrust our embodied experiences.

At Union, I was surrounded by queer community and learned about queer history for the first time. I discovered that real community looks like celebrating all parts of our multilayered selves that have been deemed unholy. I found language that fit my self-understanding, and my friends engaged in sacred acts of changing their names and their pronouns to live into their authentic selves, modeling what it means to embrace ourselves and one another in the process of self-discovery and expression. I found a community that actually felt like home—a home that was both transcendent and immanent. I found community that wasn't conditional on my own adherence to rules claimed to be "truth" and rules meant to control rather than liberate.

Queer writers like Gloria Anzaldúa, Ashon Crawley, bell hooks, Audre Lorde, and so many others, but especially my friends and the people in my community, have taken part in shaping my understanding of queerness as more than just gender and sexuality. Rather, it is a way of being that resists boundaries, categories, and limits that aim to control our bodies and what we do with them. It is about choosing to love in ways that challenge the status quo, imagining new ways of living for ourselves beyond what is imposed. Living into queerness is itself a spiritual practice.

When religious spaces become sites of ritualized violence, marginalized people have had to reimagine, and continue to reimagine, faith and community in ways that speak to them. Trans and queer people, particularly trans people of color, whose existence is impacted by multilayered and intersecting systems of oppression, have been creating homes for themselves and others outside the constructs of normative family & organized religion for centuries. They have done so by spiritualizing the material world by making their own, unique sacred spaces like drag balls and dance floors. Queer people encounter the divine through radical acts of community care; sewing and tending life amidst violence; laughing; dancing; and embodying radical abundance and expansiveness in a world that preaches scarcity and fear. For example, Sylvia Rivera and Marsha P. Johnson suffered extreme violence as trans women of color, yet both committed their lives to creating safe havens for homeless trans youth and advocating for people with HIV/AIDS. They did not just imagine a future, but they brought it into existence. These are the saints whose lives are worthy of emulation. Heaven is not some abstract concept or distant future—it is the liberation that we are tasked to create here and now on this earth for all bodies and beings.

It is specifically the bodies who get pushed out of spaces
who are told they are unworthy and unholy,
who are told there is no room for them,
who choose restoration over punishment,
who choose people over rules,
who are murdered by empire for choosing to live a life that lifts up the most vulnerable and rejects the powers that be…

These are the saints who show us the possibilities of a world we have not even imagined yet.

For all bodies that exist on the margins, who exist at crossroads, liminal and in-between spaces—these social locations move us and allow us to connect with our capacity to feel and to create new ways of surviving and thriving.

Trans and queer people are sacred, and this deep spirituality uniquely informs our world views and the ways in which we engage in storytelling in order to uplift and affirm the vitality and rawness of our existence. So, I am deeply, deeply grateful to those queer and trans, Black and Indigenous people who have come before us as well as those in our midst who are building creative pathways towards justice and liberation, who show and create us a way when there is no way. Who show me how to trust my fleshy body, a body that yearns for all bodies… to be free, to be smothered by abundant love, to know that their experience is a source of divine truth, and to know that they are altogether worthy, sacred, and beautiful.

* * *

**Carly Reiner (they/she)** is a queer, nonbinary skaterboi from Tampa currently living in East Harlem, NYC. They recently graduated with a Master of Divinity from Union Theological Seminary and a Master of Social Work from Columbia University. They love cracking open a cold one with the boys, their cat Oliver, and spending intentional time with their loved ones!

# Towards a Queer Buddhist Hermeneutics: Reparative Readings of Queer and Trans Buddhist Histories

**Kody Muncaster**
**(they/them)**

Queerness in Buddhism is an evolving debate that ranges from claims of neutrality to explicit support, to homophobia. This paper begins by discussing the current landscape of existing work on gay people in Buddhist hermeneutics and in liturgical linguistics. The paper discusses such interpretations in relation to cultural values and deconstructs the silences on issues such as femmephobia, the hatred of femininity, and interphobia, discrimination against intersex people. A queer Buddhist hermeneutics is then explored, examining Mahāyāna sutras, which are canonical scriptures that guide a later form of Buddhism, and the work of Shantideva. Finally, consideration is given to the contemporary state of queer people in Buddhism in diverse cultures.

Debates related to the appropriate use of language inevitably come up in historical discussions of queerness and often these debates derail attempts to understand queer as historical. Jose Muñoz, a scholar in queer of color critique, builds on existing literature arguing that we must maintain queerness as an expectation when reading through his examination of how queerness is ephemeral, leaving few traces that are sufficient to reach the threshold of evidence to cisgender, heterosexual eyes (Muñoz, 2019: 72). Queer existence is always historically debated due to shifts in cultural and linguistic developments, though the existence of heterosexuality is never up for debate. French philosopher Michel Foucault (1990: 101) in his groundbreaking work, *History of Sexuality: Volume* 1, explains how the modern category of homosexual was discursively constructed as a psychiatric category of being beginning in the Victorian era. While the term may have been a more recent development that preceded the term heterosexuality, the epistemic violence of erasing queerness from Buddhist historiography on the basis of language, or even because contemporary notions of gay domesticity may have looked different back then, does Buddhist studies a disservice.

It is necessary to unearth the diverse meanings of Pāḷi terms commonly examined in Buddhist hermeneutical debates on queer communities. Buddhist scholar Zwilling (1992: 205) argues that the word '*paṇḍaka*' is used in the Vinaya, the monastic rules, to refer to gay men in a so-called "passive" role, those who are effeminate, and so-called "transvestites." It is valuable to unpack these claims. The euphemistic word "passive" for what gay communities call "bottoming" is itself not neutral and implies a femininity to the so-called "receiver," as if one passively accepts the sex.

The term "effeminacy" in English is used exclusively to describe a seemingly misplaced femininity in men, with the implication that such femininity is inappropriate and indicative of gay male desire. There may be a claim that there was nothing wrong with being gay, it is just those who are feminine who are problematized. Yet, can we pause to consider: should Buddhists then not care about the suffering of feminine men? This femmephobia can be understood as a marriage between homophobia and misogyny, with the threat of being a labeled *paṇḍaka* potentially acting as a whip to ensure that men do not transgress cultural norms around masculinity.

The term "transvestite" has historically been used in English to describe non-transgender identifying men who temporarily don women's clothing, but it is unclear if this is what Zwilling meant, and they may have been referring to transwomen or trans people in general. Zwilling discusses five kinds of *paṇḍakas*:

men who give oral sex to other men and ingesting their semen (*āsita-paṇḍaka*), voyeurs, congenitally impotent men, those who have been castrated, and men who can only get aroused two weeks in the month (Zwilling, 1992: 204). There is also discussion of the female *paṇḍaka* (Harvey, 2000: 414), the term *itthipaṇḍakā* is occasionally used to mean a woman lacking in femininity and Zwilling (1992: 207) explains that two nuns are not allowed to sleep in the same bed together.

A story in the Paṇḍakavatthu section of the Theravadin Mahāvagga from the Vinaya Pitaka, which is a collection of rules that guide monastics, cited in Zwilling (1992: 207-208) discusses a gay monk who made a sexual pass at other monks, novices, along with elephant keepers, and gatekeepers. The only ones who accepted the monk's pass were the latter groups of laymen, who later mocked the monks for spending time with a *paṇḍaka*. The story claims that the Buddha later banned *paṇḍakas* from ordaining and expelled those already part of the monastic order. While one could argue that this story has to do with promiscuity, such positions are value-laden statements, which instead demonstrate about how monogamy is read into situations where it has no relevance.

While the term *paṇḍaka* has multiple meanings, this reference demonstrates an explicit banning of gay men. Buddhist scholar Gombirch (2009: 176) discusses a story of two of Shāriputra's male students having sex. Since they were not expelled from the monastic order, Gombrich (2009: 176) assumes that the act was mutual masturbation, though the Buddha did subsequently forbid a monk from having two novices at the same time, with later exceptions. This also reveals a hierarchy of what is seen to count as sex, with mutual masturbation on the lower end. This hierarchy may not be limited to Gombirch's mind. Zwilling (1992: 207) points out that gay sex is sometimes seen as less serious than heterosexual sex, as it will not lead to a monk abandoning the order to raise children. This may appear gay affirming, but it also discounts gay sex as somehow less legitimate than heterosexual sex. The widespread variance in how the term *paṇḍaka* is used puts the legitimacy of such stories in question.

The term *ubhatobyañjanaka* refers to intersex people who have also faced discrimination in Buddhism (Harvey, 2000: 413). The Upāsakaśīla-Sūtra, states that one cannot even take the lay precepts if one is "a hermaphrodite or one without sexual organs" (Heng-ching Shih, 1994: 76), hermaphrodite being an outdated term for intersex people. If intersex communities are, by extension, banned from monastic ordination on the basis that it is unclear if they would be monks or nuns, such interphobic practices are likely grounded in the heteronormative assumption that monks should live with other monks and vice-versa to prevent heterosexual encounters, erasing queer sex and disallowing the possibility for intersex people to choose where they live. It is hard to believe that, in a tradition that emphasizes compassion, the Buddha would have limited the ability for one to take precepts and by extension limited their progress on the path to enlightenment, because of their genitals, their gender, or whom they sleep with.

It may appear irrelevant to discuss trans, intersex, and gay communities in the same paper when gender, sex, and sexuality have often been written about in feminist thought as two different concepts, but understanding contemporary coalitional queer activism allows for a conceptualization of such an undertaking as necessary to fully unearth the workings of homophobia, transphobia, and interphobia. Contemporary activism uses the term 'queer' as an umbrella and a non-specific identity label for a larger community, implying that there is a relationship between the ways that people under this umbrella are oppressed. Various acronyms exist, one common acronym that is relevant here is lesbian, gay, bisexual, transgender, and intersex (LGBTI). In earlier gender and sexuality studies, gender was seen as referring to one's identity, sex to one's organs and chromosomes, and sexuality to one's orientation toward certain genders; even these distinctions have been problematized, the lines between this trinary blurred. It would be cruel to write, for example, that

Buddhism accepts masculine, celibate gay men and leave it at that without problematizing the femmephobia, interphobia, and transphobia present in these texts. Indeed, femme gay men, trans people, and intersex people have often been left out of explorations of violence in Buddhism, mentioned solely in the context of assuring masculine, celibate gay men that it is not them who terms like '*paṇḍaka*' refer to.

The question of sexual misconduct becomes a complicated one for Buddhist hermeneutics as it is confined to the narrow interpretations of a text's commentator, and those commentating on Buddhist literature rarely engage in the contemporary practice of reflexive contemplation of the influence of their culturally informed subject position on their work. In the 4th century CE, Indian monk-scholar Vasubhandu argued that oral and anal sex constituted sexual misconduct for lay people, which, by extension, eliminates the possibility of religiously condoned gay male and lesbian sex (Corless, 1998: 329). Buddhist teacher Gampopa broadened this to include having sex near a religious site, where people gather, in daylight, more than five times in a row, and with a male or with one who is castrated (Corless, 1998: 254).

The texts explored above suggest that despite attempts to argue that Buddhism has been neutral on homosexuality (see, for example, Cabezón, 1993: 82), there has been a history of exclusionary practices towards queer people. Contemporary Buddhist scholar José Cabezón concedes that Buddhist neutrality does not equate to cultural neutrality on queerness; while this point is quite relevant to many of the issues discussed above, there are still claims that the Buddha banned *paṇḍakas* from ordination (Zwilling, 1992: 207-208). Despite this, there are also texts that affirm queer identities and practices. It may take the development of a new subfield of Buddhist studies and queer studies to provide a comprehensive overview of traces of queerness in historical texts when, in homophobic times, queerness is ephemeral. While such a comprehensive examination is beyond the limits of this paper, it is necessary to begin the work of developing a queer Buddhist hermeneutics, a study of Buddhist literature that expects queerness, is done from a queer lens, and sees a queer potentiality in Buddhist texts.

Such a field must not fall prey to the trap of excessive criticism that has plagued queer theory; thus, queer theorist Eve Sedgwick's (2003) work on paranoid and reparative reading is germane. Sedgwick explains that queer theory has been dominated by an overly critical perspective that she terms 'paranoid reading.' Sedgwick explains that paranoid reading consists of five practices: (1) it is anticipatory, maintaining a future-oriented hypervigilance that attempts to prevent unexpected, negative surprises, (2) it is mimetic, requiring its own scholarly imitation and understanding only imitations of its methods, (3) it is a strong theory, teachable, and tautological, (4) it is a theory of negative affects, driven by an anxiety that seeks to maximize literary pleasure and minimize pain, and (5) paranoia places its faith in the exposure of a supposed hidden, negative meaning. Indeed, a queer Buddhist hermeneutics could fall prey to this, always anticipating hidden queerphobia. While such queerphobia must be unveiled, it can be productive to seek hidden queerness as well. Sedgwick explains another possibility in reading practices:

> To read from a reparative position is to surrender the knowing, anxious paranoid determination that no horror, however apparently unthinkable, shall ever come to the reader *as new*; to a reparatively positioned reader, it can seem realistic and necessary to experience surprise. Because there can be terrible surprises, however, there can also be good ones. (Sedgwick, 2003, p. 146, emphasis in original).

Rather than exchanging paranoid reading for reparative practices, Sedgwick argues we must diversify reading in queer studies. The two types of reading can go in tandem with one another, paranoid reading can also have reparative consequences. Sedgwick's call for reparative reading allows for there to be space for critique and praise of positive qualities. This paper began by examining the struggles of queer people in Buddhism; now it is necessary to unearth the surprising queer potentiality of Buddhist texts through a queer Buddhist hermeneutics.

Applying a queer Buddhist hermeneutics to the Vimalakīrti Sutra allows for an understanding of the queer potentiality of this sutra. Shāriputra, one of the top disciples of the Buddha, speaks to a Goddess, asking her why she does not transition from a female body to a male one. She explains that she has searched for her female form for 12 years and has not found it. Then she uses her supernatural powers to transform Shāriputra into a woman and she takes Shāriputra's form. She asks Shāriputra why Shāriputra does not change out of their female body. Shāriputra is perplexed. The goddess then explains, "the Buddha teaches that all phenomena are neither male nor female" (Watson, 1997: 91). While this sutra can be used to validate feminist goals of having women treated equally in Buddhism, it also holds a queer and trans potentiality. Cypress Atlas (2019, p. 53) examines the potential for this sutra to be read in a trans context, allowing for an understanding of nonbinary identities as an expression of emptiness. There is also the potential for a less obvious reading of this text as affirming gay identity.

We might recall Zwilling's (1992: 205) assertion that the word '*paṇḍaka*,' can be related to effeminate men due to the notion that *paṇḍakas* are *napuṃsaka* (lacking maleness). It is important to caution that such a translation is eerily close to contemporary Western stereotypes of gay men, and thus, may teach us less about a language used 2,500 years ago and more about the culture that Zwilling grew up in. However, if we are to indulge this possibility for a moment, what is less effeminate than a man who is transformed into a woman, even temporarily and not of his own will? Contemporary hegemonic masculinity can be so fragile that a hint of femininity can be sufficient evidence to others that a man is gay. While a paranoid approach would belabor criticism of Shāriputra's misogyny, a reparative reading might acknowledge the problematic sexism while also asking:

does a temporary experiment with drag make him a *paṇḍaka*? If not, is there any evidence in the texts of how effeminacy is measured to determine what makes one feminine enough to reach the threshold of *paṇḍaka*? If there is neither male nor female, then this concept of *paṇḍaka*, the definition of which seems impossible to narrow down, is empty of inherent existence; it is a linguistic, dualistic construction that has been repeatedly weaponized to justify Buddhist queerphobia. We now have an opportunity to retool this concept to read queerness in Buddhist literature.

We see a similar trans affirming and feminist message in the Devadatta chapter of the Lotus Sutra (Reeves, 2008: 247-254). The bodhisattva Manjushrī claims that the eight-year old daughter of a dragon king has attained Buddhahood. Shāriputra denies this, claiming that women are not capable of enlightenment. The dragon king's daughter appears and presents a jewel to Shakyamuni Buddha. She then transitions to male and becomes a Buddha. There are many ways of interpreting this story. A solely paranoid reading of this sutra could understand it as arguing that women cannot be enlightened without transitioning to male. Calling such a reading paranoid does not mean that there is not sexism in the sutra or that feminist critique is paranoia—in fact, the term "paranoid reading" may not be the greatest term here due to the affect behind the word "paranoid". Indeed, there is a certain misogyny to the story; however, solely occupying this critique does not allow for additional possibilities. Reparative reading allows for an intersectional feminist view, a feminist view that considers the interlocking identities that may be at play in this story. The sutra could be read as affirming trans possibilities, honoring the potential for the dragon child as a transgender person to become enlightened. We see a similar claim in the work of the eighth century CE Buddhist monk and scholar Shantideva at Bca.X.30, where he wishes "may all those in the world as women make progress, becoming men" (p. 141). While this is likely due to misguided cultural beliefs about women's apparent inability to achieve enlightenment, or even, perhaps Shantideva's own interpretation of the Lotus Sutra story above, it also normalizes notions of gender transition, even if he means being reborn as a man in one' s future lives. It is possible that texts like these could be read as both sexist and trans-affirming simultaneously. Reparative reading is steeped in an affect of hope (Sedgwick, 2003, p. 146), in this case, it is hope that despite the ephemerality of queerness in the archives, traces of queerness can still be captured in Buddhist texts.

Avalokitesvara, the bodhisattva of compassion, has become a queer icon due to its diverse depictions as male, female, both, and neither. A bodhisattva is someone who dedicates themselves to achieving infinite wisdom and compassion so that they can become a Buddha and benefit all sentient beings as opposed to a different Buddhist path, the arhat path, where one attains awakening primarily for one's own benefit. While there are people training on the bodhisattva path across the world, there are also celestial bodhisattvas, such as Avalokitesvara whose qualities Buddhists aspire to. Trans Buddhist Enke Finn discusses how Avalokitesvara has been honored as a trans or gender fluid bodhisattva (Finn, 2019: 6).

In Tibet along with some Theravada countries, Avalokitesvara is typically depicted as male whereas in East Asian countries such as China, Korea, and Japan they are represented as female. Feminist scholar Cathryn Bailey (2009, p. 178) discusses how Avalokitesvara enables a questioning of gender essentialism as their diverse depictions disrupt binary notions of gender. Bailey (2009: 179) dispels the myth that Avalokitesvara was depicted as male in India in the early Common Era and then was depicted as female in East Asia due to an East Asian association of compassion with the feminine, explaining that this is not accurate as compassion was seen as a masculine quality in China.

There is also such a diversity of Buddhist art in various countries that it is odd to imagine the bodhisattva being only depicted as one gender or another in a certain geographic location; art may be displayed from multiple countries in a single temple. She explains that Avalokitesvara is also depicted as androgynous and continues to be depicted as male as well as female today (Bailey, 2009: 192). The Lotus Sutra echoes the notion that Avalokitesvara's genders has less to do with culture and more to do with an inherent fluidity. Inexhaustible Mind Bodhisattva asked the Buddha, "World-Honored One, why does Regarder of the Cries of the World Bodhisattva travel around in this world? How does he teach the Dharma for the sake of the living? What sort of power of skillful means does he have?" (Reeves, 2008: 373). Shakyamuni Buddha replies by explaining how Avalokitesvara transforms their body to appear in any form that a person seeking help most needs. The Buddha states: "for those who need someone in the body of a boy or girl in order to be saved, he appears as a boy or girl and teaches the Dharma for them" (Reeves, 2008: 374).

Having traced queerness through Buddhist history, a consideration of the contemporary status of queer people in Buddhism is germane. Rainbodhi is an Australian-based organization dedicated to the promotion of queer people in Buddhism, founded by queer Theravada monk Bhante Akāliko. The organization sponsored research conducted by Stephen Kerry (2021, n.p.) on Australian Buddhist communities, who conducted an online survey of 82 queer and trans Buddhists in Australia and presented the results at the first International Queer Buddhist Conference in 2021. The survey found that 61% of respondents felt that Buddhist centers silence or ignore lesbian, gay, bisexual, transgender, intersex, and asexual (LGBTQIA) issues and 55% were reluctant to disclose their identities (Kerry, 2021, n.p.). In addition, 37% had seen or heard homophobia, 26% had seen or heard transphobia or misgendering, and 16% had been told that their identities were inconsistent with the Buddhist teachings (Kerry, 2021, n.p.). Scholar Coleman (2001) argues that "most teachers simply ignored the more sexist elements of the [Eastern] tradition" (p. 144)" when Buddhism came to the

West. On the contrary, researcher Kerry's data found that 54% of respondents had seen or heard sexism.

Scholar Roger Corless (2004) argues for a Western queer dharmology that examines the queer potentiality of Buddhist concepts such as *śūnyatā* (emptiness) and dependent arising. Buddhist scholar Ann Gleig (2012: 199) points out that the work of Western Buddhist scholars such as Corless propagates the view that the West is fertile ground for queer Buddhism while painting Asian Buddhism as always and only homophobic and Asian Buddhists as always and only heterosexual. Such notions are symptomatic of what queer theorist Jasbir Puar (2017: 226-227) calls a temporality of homonationalism in her description of the modern tendency to co-opt queer legal equalities as a barometer of a nation's progressiveness, enhancing the reputation of countries in the Global North while justifying imperialism on the basis of civilizing the imagined homophobic Other. Gleig (2021: 199) explains that contrary to Corless' claims, Western Buddhists tend to co-opt non-dual philosophy as a means of erasing queer and trans identities.

Cabezón (1993: 82) explains that given the diverse influences of various cultures on Buddhist perspectives on queerness, "it makes no sense to speak of a single Buddhist position as regards same-sex relations. This makes it necessary to be clear concerning the historical period and geographical location being discussed." There are historical accounts of queerness in East Asian Buddhism. Crompton (2003: 222) argues that Chinese Buddhism likely held queerness in a positive light and explains how Jesuit missionary Francis Xavier observed the practice of male love in a Zen monastery (Crompton, 2003: 413). Cabezón (1993: 92) argues that gay sex and love among monks was seen as a means of preventing monks from marrying. Cabezón explains that in Japan, gay sex was extolled as "the greatest source of sexual pleasure available to man (Cabezón, 1993: 91). Cabezón goes on to explain a story called *Chigo Kannon Engi* in which Avalokitesvara rewards a hardworking monk with a handsome male lover, which turns out to be Avalokitesvara themself (Cabezón, 1993: 91). Cabezón dispels the myth that gay sex was an outlet for celibate monks in Japanese Buddhism, as such suppositions do not explain why gay relationships held such an idealized status and this occurred during a time in which married priesthood was often practiced rather than celibacy (Cabezón, 1993: 92).

In the Tibetan Buddhist context, the Dalai Lama has issued contradictory statements on queer equality that may suggest his views are evolving. Writer Dennis Conkin (1998: 351-356) in his chapter in *Queer Dharma*, explains how in a 1994 interview with *Out Magazine*, the Dalai Lama originally stated that oral sex was wrong, but then said that if one does not have religious vows against it and if both companions agree then it is okay (Conkin, 1998: 351). The Dalai Lama did acknowledge that we can also understand the precepts in the context of temporality and culture and stated that it is "wrong for society to reject people on the basis of their sexual orientation" and "it is wrong for anyone to look down on people" (Conkin, 1998: 354). In Tibet, gay sexual practices have been documented amongst monks who engaged in physical labour known as lDab ldob (Cabezón, 1993: 93).

There have been some cases of rather affirming practices in Buddhism. Writer Jeff Wilson (2021: 31) explains that ministers of the Buddhist Churches of America (BCA), a group of Jodo Shinshu Pure Land organizations, have been performing gay marriages for nearly 50 years, well before such marriages were legalized in the United States and Canada. Buddhism does not place an emphasis on marriage and historically the Buddha did not prescribe a ceremony or a set of rituals regarding marriage, instead canonical Buddhism would view marriage as a secular affair. While gay marriage has become prominent in gay activism, particularly following the height of the AIDS pandemic, it has been met with some internal backlash. Many queer thinkers have called gay marriage an expression of homonormativity, or a means of assimilating into heterosexual institutions and wasting activist energy that could be better spent on structural issues (Puar, 2006: 73; Conrad, 2014: 57). Anti-assimilationist critiques argue that the benefits of marriage such as having a spouse be able to visit one in the hospital, easing immigration for a partner, and allowing access to health insurance for one's spouse, should actually be available to all people regardless of marital status, thus marriage equality privileges those who chose this legal route and leaves behind those who do not. While the BCA's choice to conduct gay marriages may be a kind gesture of affirming and welcoming queers into its churches, it also acts as a sort of dual assimilation: assimilating Buddhism into Christian notions of religious marriage in the West and assimilating queers into homonormative marriage, calming the fires of their activism once they have attained the rights (when legalized) of other married couples.

While the Buddha did have a wife before he began his journey into Buddhahood, there is precedent for understanding the Buddha as bisexual. Cabezón (1993: 89) explains that Ānanda and the Buddha are depicted as lovers in the Jataka tales, stories of the Buddha's past lives. In one story, the Buddha and Ānanda are two deer who spend their lives cuddling each other. In another, they are sons of Brahmin parents, and they refuse to marry women so that they can be with each other instead. Given that the Buddha married a woman in his historical life before his spiritual journey, was the Buddha bisexual? Perhaps by today's standards. Even if celibacy prevented the Buddha and Ānanda from having sex in their historical life, it is possible that a gay loving, romantic relationship was present. The Buddha is said to have had the ability to see his own past lives and the Jataka tales were narrated directly by the Buddha to his followers with lessons on the path to Buddhahood, so while the Buddha was alive he would have told these stories about his romantic relationship with Ānanda in a past life—denoting a present bisexual-romantic connection even if sex was out of the picture in that particular lifetime. There is often a fear of applying an anachronistic label to people in another time period, yet heterosexuality is seen in historiography as such a given that it does not even need to be labeled. Queerness is so ephemeral that we are desperate for traces of people like us in our histories, thus, such a label for the sake of ease in rendering our love and sex intelligible to contemporary discursive sensibilities can only serve to benefit beings.

Ānanda expressed a profound amount of love for the Buddha during his historical life and experienced an incredible magnitude of mourning when the Buddha died. In Volume 2 of *Queer Dharma*, writer Michael J. Sweet (2000: 15) quotes a verse attributed to Ānanda after the Buddha's death:

> My companion has passed away,
> The Master, too, is gone.
> There is no friendship now that equals this:
> Mindfulness directed to the body.
> The old ones now have passed away,
> The new ones do not please me much,
> Today I meditate all alone
> Like a bird gone to its nest. (Thag. 1035-1036).

The profound grief expressed in this passage may be that of a widower. Ānanda makes a point of calling the Buddha his companion while also acknowledging him as The Master of the Dharma. Author Sweet (2000: 14) explains that Ānanda's attachment to the Buddha was so great that he could only attain the spiritual level of arhatship after the Buddha died.

Ānanda is also depicted in a past life as falling in love with a jeweled neck snake that appeared in a male human form. The jeweled neck would visit Ānanda in his hermitage in human form and then transform into his snake form to hug Ānanda tight when it was time for him to leave. The jeweled neck would not remain at Ānanda's hermitage until he had "sineham vinodetvā," which Sweet (2000: 17) translates as meaning released his sticky love fluid. Ānanda begins to wish to leave the relationship, and his brother advises him to ask the jeweled neck for money, appearing as a gold-digger to make him leave. When the jeweled neck leaves, Ānanda is ridden with guilt, regretting the decision. His brother concludes that Ānanda cannot live without the jeweled neck. Sweet (2000: 18) relates this to the phrase "boyfriends, can't live with em, can't live without em." Sweet (2000: 18) explains that this story could be arguing for the merits of non-attached, ascetic life, or perhaps it is an approval of gay romance, drawing the line at gay sex. Perhaps it could even be a story of Ānanda's internalized homophobia, his running away from a gay relationship and then later missing his lover, an experience that is all too familiar in queer communities.

Buddhism and its perspectives on gender and sexuality are diverse, in flux, and largely dependent on culture, time period, and who is translating a text. These factors make it impossible to articulate a pan-Buddhist perspective on queerness or to provide a dualistic yes or no answer to questions of whether Buddhism endorses queer and trans identities. Using a queer Buddhist hermeneutics, it is evident that there is much justification in the texts for affirming queer and trans communities and at the same time, cultural homophobia has led to problematic interpretations of Buddhist literature. While one could use a queer Buddhist hermeneutics to conclude that Buddhism embraces queerness, one must balance this with a consideration of the often challenging lived reality of queers in Buddhist communities. It is also important to note that the language that the Buddha spoke is highly debated and some argue that it was an earlier dialect close to Pāḷi that that the Buddha spoke rather than Pāḷi itself (Levman, 2019: 53). While the Pāḷi Canon is seen as closest to the original teachings of the Buddha, we can recognize that it was written down hundreds of years after the Buddha's death and thus it is unfortunately impossible to know the authenticity of stories about paṇḍakas. Regardless, it behooves engaged Buddhists to remember that the Buddha's teachings on lovingkindness and compassion must be extended to all beings, including those queer, trans, femme, and intersex people who are currently suffering under the oppression of homophobia, transphobia, femmephobia, and interphobia in their Buddhist communities.

* * *

## References

Atlyss, Cypress. (2019). "Gender and Emptiness." in *Transcending: Trans Buddhist Voices*. Edited by Kevin Manders and Elizabeth Marston. Berkeley: North Atlantic Books

Bailey, Cathryn. (2009) "Embracing the Icon: The Feminist Potential of the Trans Bodhisattva, Kuan Yin." *Hypatia* 24, no. 3: 178-196.

Cabezón, J.I. (1993). 'Homosexuality and Buddhism', in A. Swidler, ed., *Homosexuality and World Religions*, Valley Forge, Penn., Trinity Press International, pp.81-101.

Coleman, J. W. (2001). *The New Buddhism: The Western Transformation of an Ancient Tradition*. London: Oxford University Press.

Conkin, Dennis. (1998). "The Dalai Lama and Gay Love" *Queer Dharma: Voices of Gay Buddhists, Volume 1*, edited by Winston Leyland, pp.351-56. Gay Sunshine Press.

Conrad, R. ed. (2014). *Against Equality: Queer Revolution, Not Mere Inclusion*. AK Press.

Corless, Roger. (1998) "Coming out in the Sangha: Queer Community in American Buddhism," in Prebish, C. S. and Tanaka, K. K., (eds) *The Faces of Buddhism in America*. London: University of California Press, pp. 253 - 265.

Crompton, L. (2003) *Homosexuality & Civilization*. Cambridge and London: The Belknap Press of Harvard University Press.

Crosby, Kate, & Skilton, Andrew. (2008). *Santideva The Bodhicaryavatara: New Translation* by Kate Crosby and Andrew Skilton. Oxford University Press.

Enke, Finn. (2009). "What is a Body, Anyway? Form, Deep Listening, and Compassion on a Buddhist Trans Path" in *Transcending: Trans Buddhist Voices*. Edited by Kevin Manders and Elizabeth Marston. Berkeley: North Atlantic Books.

Foucault, M. (1990). *The History of Sexuality: An Introduction*. Vintage.

Gleig, Ann. (2012). "Queering Buddhism or Buddhist De-Queering? Reflecting on Differences Amongst Western LGBTQI Buddhists and the Limits of Liberal Convert Buddhism." *Theology & Sexuality*, *18*(3), pp.198-214.

Gombrich, Richard. (2009). *What the Buddha Thought*. London and Oakville: Equinox.

Harvey, Peter. (2000). *An Introduction to Buddhist Ethics: Foundations, Values and Issues*. Cambridge University Press.

Hạnh, Thich Nhất. (2020). *Interbeing: The 14 Mindfulness Trainings of Engaged Buddhism*. Berkeley: Parallax Press.

Kerry, S. (2021). Australian LGBTQIA+ Buddhists, 1-27. Paper presented at 1st International Queer Buddhist Conference.

Levman, B. (2019). "The Language the Buddha Spoke" *Journal of the Oxford Centre for Buddhist Studies,* 17.

Muñoz, José Esteban. (2019). *Cruising Utopia: The Then and There of Queer Futurity*. NYU Press, 72.

Puar, J.K. (2006). "Mapping US Homonormativities." *Gender, Place & Culture*, *13*(1), pp. 67-88.

Puar, Jasbir K. (2018). *Terrorist Assemblages: Homonationalism in Queer Times*. Duke University Press.

Reeves, G. (2008). *The Lotus Sutra*. Boston, MA: Wisdom.

Sedgwick, Eve Kosofsky. (2003). *Touching Feeling: Affect, Pedagogy, Performativity*. Duke University Press.

Sweet, Michael, J. (1998). "Pining Away for the Sight of the Handsome Cobra King: Ananda as Gay Ancestor and Role Model." In *Queer Dharma: Voices of Gay Buddhists, Volume 2*, edited by Winston Leyland pp. 13-24. Gay Sunshine Press.

Watson, B. (1997). *The Vimalakirti Sutra.* Columbia University Press. Beyond Worship 132.

Wilson, J. (2012). "All Beings are Equally Embraced by Amida Buddha": Jodo Shinshu Buddhism and Same-sex Marriage in the United States. *Journal of Global Buddhism*, 13, pp. 31-59.

Zwilling, L. (1992). "Homosexuality as Seen in Indian Buddhist Texts." In *Buddhism, Sexuality, and Gender,* edited by J. I. Cabezón, 203-214. Albany: SUNY Press.

* * *

**Kody Muncaster (they/them)** is both a PhD Candidate in Gender, Sexuality, and Women's Studies at Western University and a MA student in Buddhist Studies at the University of South Wales. Their research and consulting interests include engaged Buddhism, mindfulness-based psychotherapy, HIV/AIDS, queer suicide, and trauma.

# RESPONSES & RITUALS

## A Ritual for LGBTQIA+ Survivors of Religious Trauma

**By Ellie Hutchison Cervantes, M.Div.**
**(she/her)**

Conservative, fundamentalist, and otherwise toxic religious environments can cause significant and lasting harm. Such religious spaces often demand submission and conformity; reinforce traditional gender roles; stigmatize the body and sexuality; and assert homophobic, transphobic, and sexist beliefs. To violate these beliefs and norms often fosters shame (an inherent sense that one is "bad" or "wrong"), the impulse to hide or suppress parts of one's identity (such as one's sexuality), and it risks one's belonging within the community. These characteristics can make toxic religious spaces particularly traumatizing for LGBTQIA+ people.

Rituals can help us acknowledge the suffering we have experienced, honor the grief and pain associated with our trauma, and begin to process and heal from it. Because rituals are active, embodied practices, they can also help counteract the loss of agency and disconnection from the self that often results from trauma.

**PREPARE**

- Choose your company. Consider if there is a trusted friend or small group you could invite to participate in this ritual with you.
- Choose a time to engage in the ritual in which you won't be rushed.
- Choose a place where you feel safe and comfortable, and where you won't be easily distracted or interrupted.

- Gather materials:
  - A candle
  - A loose piece of paper (uncolored and non-glossy), a writing utensil, and scissors
  - If you are able to safely integrate fire into the ritual, then locate a fire-safe receptacle, such as an outdoor fire pit, a fireplace, a cooking pot, or metal or glass bowl. Also bring a lighter, pitcher of water, and metal tongs.
  - Decide what else might support you in this ritual, such as incense or essential oils (consider using rosemary or sage), a picture of your younger self, a cherished object from childhood, or other resources from your religious or ancestral traditions.

**ENTER**

- When you are ready to begin, thoughtfully arrange the materials you've gathered. Create a different atmosphere for the room you are in by turning down the lights, turning off phones and screens, and making other adjustments as needed. Light your candle.
- Ground yourself by connecting with the present moment, the space you inhabit, and your body. Sometimes connecting with your breath and body can be triggering, so be mindful of this and adjust your practice accordingly. Take the time you need to move through the following steps:
  - Observe your surroundings. Notice the physical space you are in and remember the land you are on. Consider how the earth is supporting you right now.
  - Place a hand on your heart. Notice your heartbeat. Remember that you are here and alive. Consider all that your body is quietly doing to sustain you in this moment.

    - Notice your breath. Follow the air as it enters your nostrils, fills your lungs, and then leaves your body again. Continue to breathe at an easy, natural pace for a few minutes.
- Set an intention for the ritual.
    - Possible intentions could be to:
        - Release false beliefs that you've internalized
        - Connect with your younger self and offer them compassion
        - Grieve the suffering and injustices that you've experienced in religious communities
    - State your intention out loud and invite the spirit of Love to meet you in this moment.
- As you move into the core of the ritual, keep in mind that rituals often create space for feelings, sensations, memories, and other stimuli to arise—especially those that are unprocessed and have been repressed or dismissed in the past. I encourage you to notice what may come up, consider why it is arising, and take the time you need to tend to it. You can return to your breath whenever you need a moment of calm or grounding.

**RELEASE**

- As you feel safe and able to do so, bring to mind the religious environments in which you were harmed; perhaps it was a particular religious community, a leader or mentor you trusted, a sacred text, a religious tradition or practice, or a set of beliefs. Consider what you experienced, how it shaped you, and how it continues to inform who you are and how you move through the world.

  You can use the following questions as prompts for reflection if they resonate with you. You may also find it helpful to reflect silently, by journaling, or through verbal processing.

  - How has religion harmed me? In what ways am I still wounded by this?
  - What was I told about myself, my sexuality, and my body-mind-spirit that I now recognize is untrue?
  - What life-limiting beliefs have I internalized?
  - When I think about what I have experienced and survived, what do I need to grieve?
- On the left side of a loose sheet of paper, write down the lies and false beliefs that you wish to release. Put each one on a new line *(ex. I am sinful).*
- Next, on the right side of the paper, write down a truth or affirmation that counters these lies. Create an alternative, empowering narrative that can serve as an antidote to what you were taught *(ex. I am sacred).*
- Rip the sheet in half, down the center, to divide the lies from the truths.
- Now, rip or cut up the left half of the paper that has the false beliefs on it into individual pieces, so that each one is on its own slip of paper.
  - If you are able to safely burn these slips of paper, proceed through the following steps:
    - Place your pitcher of water, metal tongs, and candle next to your fire-safe receptacle.
    - Grab one of the pieces of paper with your tongs and burn it in the candle's flame. As it burns, recite these words: *"I release ______"* followed by your new affirmation. (ex. *"I release the belief that I am sinful. I affirm that I am sacred."*)
    - Drop the burning piece of paper in the receptacle, pour water over it, and then repeat the process with the next slip of paper until you are done.
  - If you are unable to safely burn the pieces of paper, then simply rip or cut up each of them.
    - As you do so, recite the words: *"I release ______"* followed by your new affirmation. "(ex.

*"I release the belief that I am sinful. I affirm that I am sacred."*)

- You can save these pieces of paper to burn later, you can bury them in the earth, or you can recycle them.

**CLOSE**

- To close, read your list of new affirmations aloud to yourself as a final blessing. Hold onto this list and consider displaying it somewhere, like on a mirror or in your journal, so it can serve as an ongoing reminder of the truth.
- When you are finished, offer gratitude to yourself for showing up and pursuing healing today. Give thanks for all that supported you as you engaged in this ritual. Celebrate the brilliance and beauty of who you are now, honoring all you have endured and survived to reach this moment in your life.

**FOLLOW UP**

Suggested Steps for Self-Care and Integration

- Immediately after the ritual, connect with the element of water in some way. You could shower, bathe, or simply wash your face. As you do so, visualize the false beliefs that you've released rinsing off of you and the residue of the past being washed away.
- Reflect on your experience of the ritual and continue to process what arose for you during it. You can do this by journaling; creating art; or talking with a spiritual director, therapist, mentor, or friend.
- On an ongoing basis, engage in somatic healing modalities that are supportive of and accessible to you. Possibilities include yoga, dance, meditation, humming, singing, or stretching.
- Connect with other LGBTQIA+ folks—including those

who have also been harmed by religion and can relate to your experience. Seek out relationships and communities that joyfully embrace, celebrate, and affirm all of who you are.

* * *

**Ellie Hutchison Cervantes (she/her)** is an ace communications consultant, chaplain in training, and social justice advocate. She holds a Master of Divinity in Spiritual Care and Social Healing from Union Theological Seminary and is here to remind you that you are loved.

## Write Your Own Prayer Poem
## By Jessi-Alez Brandon
**(they/he)**

Holy ________________________, Why must I grieve with every breath I take?
(title you use for God/Spirit/Love)

The persistent presence of ______________________ weighs down my soul in
(heavy, debilitating emotion)

unsustainable ways. You are my _______________________, whose power helped me out of
(title for God/Spirit/Love)

my darkest valleys. So why am I still fighting? Why are we still fighting? You hear our

communities' cries for a better way than we have. How are we still mourning?

___________________________, as the days of fighting against ___________________________

(title for God/Spirit/Love) (oppressions hitting your heart)

grow longer and longer and ceasefires grow further and shorter in between, the urge to

______________________________ in the name of righteous ______________________________ grows
(something you struggle with) (heavy, debilitating emotion)

ever stronger. Even when it hurts to do so.

It is perfectly human to hurt. But to stay rooted for ourself and our neighbors, help our hurt

make way for healing. So now I ask You, O my ____________, lead my away
(title for God/Spirit/Love)

from ________________ and lead me to ____________________ so I can express
(something you struggle with) (name life-giving practice)

my righteous _________________________ in a way that honors You and Your
(heavy, debilitating emotion)

liberating ways. Let me draw my strength from Your ______________________________
(favorite characteristic of God/Spirit/Love)

instead of______________________ in order to give You thanks.
(heavy, debilitating emotion)

Because You feel with us, You are also tired. But You have the strength to push us forward to a world that mirrors Your just and joyful kin-dom. Thank You for Your gentle nudge to a definite better. Amen.

* * *

**Jessi-Alex Brandon (they/he)** is a Black, queer, nonbinary poet from Alabama. He identifies as Christian but strives every day to understand the Divine outside of the white evangelical frameworks he was raised in. Their poetry has been previously published by Button Poetry and Macalester College's Wordplay! Newsletter.

## Flames of Love

**Kimi Floyd Reisch**
**(they/them)**

We light the flame of commitment,
To stand with and work to create change,
Until all know they are beloved.

We light the flame of survival,
Grateful for our lives,
Remembering in love those lost along the road.

We light the flame of change,
Committing to recenter toward love,
In hearts, in minds, in our world.

We light the flame of hope,
Loving each other, building community,
even when it is uncomfortable.

We light the flame of knowledge,
Following the path of justice,
Justice that is love embodied.

We light this flame of radical love, and commit:
To speak out for those who have been silenced.
Those who have been rejected for who they love.
Those who have been persecuted for who they are.

Those who have been bullied for daring to be bold.
Those who have been othered and forced into the margins.
Those who have been lonely.
Those who have been hurt.
Those who are still hurting.

We light this flame as
a people committed,
we are survivors.
we will change the world,
until no one lives without hope,
until no one lives without justice.
We light this flame and pledge that
In love, with love, and through love,
All things are possible.

* * *

**Kimi Floyd Reisch (they/them)** is an interfaith advocate, educator, and movement builder. Kimi Floyd uses healing stories from many cultures and places to guide people to a deeper understanding of who they are and who they want to become. They earned their Master of Divinity degree at United Theological Seminary of the Twin Cities in Minnesota and are currently working on a Doctoral degree in Public Theology. As a pansexual, two-spirit person, growing up in Wyoming, they learned that hearing each other's stories is essential for mutual respect. Their faith is centered in their Siksiká, Lenape, Mahican, and Scots-Irish heritage. They are a member at City of Refuge UCC in Oakland, California, and the Director of Program Ministry at the Unitarian Universalist Santa Fe (NM). They are an authorized humanist celebrant and associate chaplain through the Humanist Society of America.

## Guided Somatic Grounding Meditations

**Oran Miller, M.Div.**
**(they/them)**

*An intentional way to drop into our body/mind/spirit and feel ourselves in connection with the power of our environment and trans/queer community.*

*prior to the exercise find a comfortable place to land, light a candle, and connect with your surroundings.

Drop in and notice how you feel right now

- Being here, in this moment, wherever you may find yourself.
- Bring your attention to the level of sensation in your body below the neck.
  - What can you feel? Is the room warm or cool? Are you experiencing anything positive or negative or neutral related to digestion? Do you feel nervous or sore? Is there any joy or grief coming up for you?
- At the time, there is nothing to fix. There is just a sense of coming into awareness to feel more and more of what might be silenced when moving through the day-to-day of life.
- For most people, the center of the body is about two inches below the belly button. If you place your hand there, can you feel what or where your body is calling you

to explore? Can you feel the exchange of energy and sensations within your body? Can you bring your awareness to this center? If your center is feeling alive in another part place of your body, feel the freedom to listen, honor it, and adjust the reflection from your center.

- This somatic exercise will call in awareness to bodily limbs that may not be present or difficult from which to access sensation. Many are not used to feeling their body in this way, so hold as much compassion and patience for yourself as possible and use your imagination to adjust to for your needs.

From here we move in 4 dimensions: Length, Width, Depth, and Longing. Then, we will move into a Mood Check.

**Length:**

- Move your awareness from the center of your body down your legs, into your feet, through the floor, dropping in further through the layers of the ground, into the water table, even deeper connecting with the core of the earth. Allow gravity to have a little more of you bit by bit. Take a moment to connect with your depth.
- Begin to bring your awareness back up through your feet and legs. Shift your awareness up your spine, through your neck, and head extending up into the sky. Can you feel your length in its entirety?
- Some link this length to our dignity. Can you feel your dignity in your length and extension?
- Take a breath and hold that dignity.
- Unfurl from your center out to your edges, where we'll center on the dimension of width.

**Width:**

- How does it feel to move from the center to the edge? From right to left?

- Width is about our right to take up space and about connection with our environments and the people around us. How do you feel your connection to others? Can you feel yourself as a part of a massive circle? Can you feel yourself as a part of a circle of connection between those you share dreams with but have never met?
- Width is about taking up space. Relax and open up in your width. Acknowledge that you have a right to be here. Can you widen yourself even more now?

**Depth:**

- Begin by moving from back to front and front to back, sternum to spine.
- Bring your awareness to your core, starting from the inside, can you soften your belly, soften your lungs, and create make more space for you to move around within your depth.
- It can help to remember that there is a back and a front of to your heart, and a back and a front of to your belly.
- To look back, extend back is to touch where we come from. We can reach our ancestry and our past experiences. What and who is at your back? Who has been a wisdom bearer for you? Who taught you about feeling good in your body? Who supports you to be here today?
- Your back knows about that. Spend a moment breathing with your back, softening and expanding. You might just feel sensation over narrative, a twinge, a tightening, a release. Just listen with your senses.
- Call upon gender expansive ancestors and all those who have come before us who inspire your becoming. Can you feel their support and love at your back?
- Coming through your body to the front, feel your face, your chest, and the front of your toes
- The front of us faces what is to come, what is ahead. Mystery unknown, and the world we can get to shape together. Do Can you feel something growing here?

- Feel yourself in this dimension, behind and ahead, holding the flux.

**Longing:**

- Lastly, we will center on what we long for, what we care about.
- Bring these longings into your center and allow them it to grow. Imagine your body filling up with your dreams and desires all the way in way to your skin to the skin, the edges of your body, your being. Spend a moment centering in your longing, desire, and values.

**Mood check:**

- Spend a moment debriefing of debrief with yourself and/or trusted others to share what has come to mind and body is coming up for you as you ground yourself and consider the context and environment in which you are grounding.
- Where are you coming from before this moment of pause? Are there any distractions or anything keeping you from being present? Are you feeling connected with your body or with a message with a message? Feeling unsettled? A jumble of things?
- All moods are welcome. There is not a better or a worse mood, a correct or an incorrect mood, there is room for all moods.
- Thank yourself for entering this space, for all information and sensations that arose, no matter the clarity. Make an intention to come back and visit the feelings that wish to be noticed.

* * *

**Oran Miller**, M.Div. (they/them), is a multidisciplinary artist and queer spiritual care companion. Their work can be found at 0rangebl0ss0m.com.

## A Queer Rite for the Affirmation of a Name
## by Pippa Charleigh Oaks
### (she/her)

*Congratulations on your name! This is a short rite of passage which can be added to the context of a community liturgy, or celebrated at a party, BBQ, casual gathering around a campfire, or wherever/whenever the vibe feels right!*

*In the following ritual, the term "Leader" is used to denote the person(s) who lead(s) the ritual. It's always a good idea to agree upon assigned roles prior to beginning in order to maintain a sense of flow throughout the rite. A highlighter or pen can be useful for marking when it's your turn to participate. Ideally everyone has an opportunity to practice reading their parts aloud beforehand.*

*Wherever you encounter "[NAME]," you will insert the name of the participant. If possible, it's nice to print out a copy with your name written in. You may want to use first name only, or include middle name and/or last name at certain points in the liturgy. This is entirely up to you.*

*Feel free to adjust the language or form of this rite to best fit your unique context. You may want to add relevant readings, special music, or significant prayers/actions/words from your religious or spiritual tradition (or from your favorite pop-culture artists).*

*If the participant will be signing any name change documents, or unveiling a new driver's license/passport/documentation, it would most naturally fit into this rite following a reading, or during a song or performance. Reminder: your name, gender, and pronouns are 100% valid regardless of any 'official' government paperwork.*

*Parenthesis (round brackets) are used throughout this rubric to indicate optional inclusion. For a participant who is also using new pronouns the phrase "and pronouns" appears in parentheses, as are gendered options like "sister," "brother," or "sibling." Sometimes words in brackets indicate alternate verbiage - choose any or all that apply.*

*Please be mindful that not all elements of this ritual will be fully accessible and modifications may be necessary. Note that chanting or raucous applause may be an overwhelming sensory experience for some, and that portion of this rite may need to be adapted to fit the needs of your particular context.*

*There is an option to include touch in this ritual in the form of a gentle hand on the shoulder at the moment of affirmation. Pre-established and ongoing consent must be established before touching another person in any/every context. When in doubt, leave touch out.*

**A Queer Rite for the Affirmation of a Name**
**Welcome and Introduction**

Leader: Throughout the ages and across many spiritual traditions there are
powerful stories of those who were gifted a new name through divine
encounter, or who chose a new name as part of their personal journey of
self-discovery (individuation, or spiritual transformation).

We have gathered here today in the spirit of our Mighty Transcestors, and
our gender-nonconforming forebears to continue the legacy of Queer

empowerment through the affirmation of a new name (and pronouns).

Names carry the power to define ourselves on our own terms.
Names locate us within our communities and relationships.
Names are a container to hold the uncontainable essence of our being.

*The leader(s) may share a short reflection(s), here.*
*The leader may then introduce optional reading(s) and/or music.*

**Reading from a relevant poem or sacred text (optional)**
*Silence may be kept for a moment following readings.*

**Special Music or Performance (optional)**
*Silence may be kept for a moment following music or a performance.*

Leader: [ NAME ] , is there anything special you would like to share with us about your name (and pronouns)?

Participant:

---

________________________________________

________________________________________

________________________________________ *

** Here's a lovely opportunity to share something personal about your new name. Maybe a story of how your name came to you, or what your name means to you, or something that invites the community to know you in a new way.*

** Some people prefer to write and read a short reflection, others like to speak freely from the heart, and still others prefer to keep this more personal and private. You could ask someone else to read something you've written out beforehand if that feels more accessible or comfortable for you. Whatever you choose, it's always helpful to communicate your preference to the leader before beginning the ritual.*

**The Rite of Affirmation**

*The leader turns to the participant and says,*

**Leader**: Thank you for inviting us to share in this rite of passage with you.
Are you ready for us to collectively affirm your name (and pronouns)?

**Participant:** I'm ready!

*Any enthusiastic indication of consent is valid, here.*

*The leader turns to the community and asks,*

**Leader:** Are we ready to collectively affirm [NAME'S] name (and pronouns)?

**All:** We're ready!
*Any enthusiastic indication of consent is valid, here.*

*The leader turns to the participant. The leader(s) may also opt to place a gentle hand on the participant's shoulder (only if consent is pre-established) and say,*

**Leader:** [ NAME ], we accept and affirm you today as a milestone in your journey
of self-discovery. Thank you for sharing this part of yourself with us. We
will honor your name (and pronouns) in your presence and safeguard
your name (and pronouns) in your absence.

*The leader begins a chant of the participant's name. It can be fun to start slowly and quietly, and build speed, volume and gusto!*

[ NAME ] ! [ NAME ] ! [ NAME ] !

**All** join in:[ NAME ] ! [ NAME ] ! [ NAME ] ! [ NAME ] ! [ NAME ] ! [ NAME ] !

*Repeat chanting the name until it feels appropriate to conclude the rite.*

**The Closing Words and Blessing**

**Leader**: Let's officially welcome [ NAME ] , our friend (and sister/brother/sibling) to the world by their name!

**All**: *Cheer! Holler! Whoop and whistle! / Clap hands! / Snap fingers!*

**Leader:** Thank you all for your presence today — truly a day for celebration!
Please take a moment to personally congratulate [NAME ] before you
head home.

*The leader(s) may raise hands towards the community in a gesture of benediction*

Be blessed by Queer Spirits and the Mighty Transcestors!

*The leader may use an additional or alternate blessing according to your spiritual or religious tradition, or may simply declare* ***"Let's Party!"***

* * *

My name's **Pippa (she/her)** – I'm a Queer, nonbinary trans woman, formerly ordained priest (Anglican, aka Episcopalian), and I'm currently working as an independent spiritual care provider for Queer and Trans people based in Toronto, Ontario (under Toronto Purchase Treaty 13 on the traditional land of the Anishinaabeg, Huron-Wendat and Petun First Nations, the Seneca, and most recently, the Mississaugas of the Credit River). My current spiritual practice is primarily informed by: (1) universalist, post-Christian mysticism, (2) animistic, Earth-based paganism drawing from my own eclectic witchcraft, (3) ceremonial magick, and (4) politicized embodiment practices for personal empowerment, communal healing, and social justice.

# BENEDICTIONS

## Be Possessed
## Nordia Bennett
### (she/they)

You say there is an evil spirit inside me that must be exorcised.
My response to you is that you are correct.
The Spirit of inauthenticity.
The Spirit of fear.
The Spirit of daring not to be powerful.
The Spirit of self-hate.
The Spirit of lack of self-esteem.
The Spirit of not loving my curves, thighs, and thickness.
The Spirit that drives me so far from my true self I scream because that person I'm in bed with hates me, despises me, and doesn't trust me.
I roll over looking her dead in the eyes and only see death, sadness, and hurt.
The evil that resides contorts, manipulates, and seizes all voluntary control she wished she possessed but allows fear to consume her.
The evil spirit you speak of burns of wasted flesh because the space I take up is pointless.
I wear a mask that feeds the evil spirit all that it needs to prosper.
It needs lies.
The lies I tell myself at night because evil has a funny way of looking more comfortable and more home than freedom.
Freedom became the darkness I dreamt of.
The evil eats away at the darkness feeding my insecurities more and more.

Freedom is the lie evil told me.
I crumble to freedom.
I am lost for words— speechless of shall I say helpless.
The evil you speak of inside me made a home and it's me.
The evil inside me creeps waiting for freedom to knock at my door, but instead I did not recognize it.
Freedom called and I declined.
For I scream to the top of my lungs but evil has a way of molding illusions. I saw freedom, but instead I was dragged and forced to drown in the tears of my broken dreams.
The dream of one day being free.
This evil has a name.
This evil you speak of— queer
Queerness
My queerness is the evil you speak of.
All I can say is thank you for you have named the thing that has set me free.
Inauthenticity is afraid of authenticity. It is afraid of queerness.
We will name the evil spirit and release it into the world for all to see and be blessed by the spirit that overcame me and introduced me to an alternative way of living that is blessed and true.
Set me free to see me for the first time in a long time.
So call that spirit forth. It will be happy you did.
I sure enough am.
My queerness stands tall— unchecked and unfiltered.
Freedom called.
Queerness called.
And this time I answered.

* * *

**Nordia Bennett (She/They)** is a preacher, writer, creator, and educator. She recently graduated with her Master of Divinity from Union Theological Seminary. Nordia believes that the revelation of God is on earth, here and now waiting to be experienced. When Nordia is not working, she enjoys iced matcha lattes and spending time with her friends.

## My beloved queer child

**Brandon Roiger**
**(they/he)**

*This benediction was written in honor of a genderqueer teenager who died by suicide. It is for all queer and transgender young people we have lost because we have failed to love their sacred queerness.*

My beloved queer child
I wish you knew how
deeply loved you are
by the queer ancestors
who came before

May you be embraced
by the stars
who even in explosion
do not know pain

May you also create
new galaxies and universes
in the spirit you leave
with queers you'll never know

Oh, even if you did not
know the deepest love
I simply hope
you now have peace

Oh, even if you did not
I hope your life
creates something
beyond this

I hope you now know love
and more than anything
I hope you
bring it back to us

In the sound of steps
no one else hears
A gust of wind
different than the others

By water once visited
with a spontaneous ripple
Through the unexplained
and the mysterious

Return to the stars now
To dust
To love
To peace

My beloved queer child
Suffer no more
Rest with the queer spirits
who always knew
who you were

* * *

**Brandon Roiger (they/he)** is an abolitionist, youth worker, chaplain, and organizer. They are centered by abolition and transformative justice as spiritual frameworks for being in relationship to others, and they seek to imagine how communities can transform the harm that young people experience under abuse, oppression, and violent interpersonal/social structures. Brandon enjoys walks in the park with a friend, running, being by water, and playing volleyball.

## Dear Moon, An Elegy

**Queerly Complex**
**(they/them)**

Dear Moon,

I cannot see you this morning as the sky is covered, and the heavens are crying. "The angels are weeping," was what I was told, "they mourn for humanity." And I believed this lie. It is no longer simply a lie. It is myth, and as I stand under your tears, I accept this myth as truth. We need you to cry, to wail, to mourn so loudly you stop all in their tracks. We are careening towards death, and your tears are life.

Can you please, please, please weep & wail & sob & keen & rain down? Can your mourning please stop humanity before we kill ourselves?

Dear Moon,

I cannot see you this morning as the sky is covered, and my tears are flowing in rhythm with yours. I imagine how your distance and age allows you to experience death not as an ending or beginning or even as part of a cycle but as the truth for which it is: Death, simply, be; Always & Everywhere; a constant in its truest sense. This truth is hard to bear and bare, and yet you do so day in and day out for all to see. I am grateful for this moment of shared rhythm for it reminds me that grieving is naturally cosmic; it connects me to you.

Is this what it means to be transformed by death? Are your appearances a remembrance to constantly be transformed by you?

Dear Moon,

I cannot see you this mourning as my eyes are covered, and my cheeks are wet with divinity. I remember the distance between my father and me as he lay dying in his bed in his home in Minnesota with his wife holding his hand and I sat in mine with my beautiful's arms around me in our home in San Francisco on December 26th, 2020. It was this distance and his death that transformed me, and I taste its salty reminder every time I cry. I am learning that this remembrance is divinity. It is you, The (Covered) Moon, who is revealing this.

What revelations will come when you are no longer covered? Who will I become when I see you fully?

Dear Moon,

I cannot see you this mourning as my eyes are covered, and my hand refuses to move. I am unsure I am ready for another transformation; it feels too soon for I have been forced to transform again and again and again and again, and I just desire some respite from your constant remembrances. But in writing these poetics I am etching your truth as a constant in my body.

Am I just afraid to accept the truth: Death is Always & Everywhere? Is this a pathway towards liberation?

Dear Moon,

I've lowered my hand, and I can now see you this morning as the clouds are beginning to part, and the rain is still falling on these parched lands. I can feel the ground drinking, taking in a big gulp of the heavens. I open my mouth, and I too drink in its pleasure. As it slides down my esophagus, I am reminded of my beautiful standing over me, swallowing his salty, bitter life. The sensation is the same, and so too is my arousal.

Is this what it feels like to be consumed by your divinity? Is this what the earth feels right now?

Dear Moon,

I can now see you this morning and this mourning for the sky is clear, and my heart is free. My pleasure in your tears and its remembrances of arousal remind me that even amidst constant death there is constant creation. There is no escaping both. You up there uncovered and beautiful is proof of creation. There was a time you did not exist and there will be a time you do not exist. For here and now, though, you live while witnessing constant death. And it is this state that creates gravity, that shifts tides, that reminds and has reminded and will remind all of humanity that there is something greater than ourselves, our being.

How best can I be a herald of your truth?

In grief & joy & rage & love,
Queerly Complex

* * *

**Queerly Complex (they/them)** is an anti-binary social practice artist living & creating on Yelamu, unceded Ramaytush Ohlone land, aka San Francisco. A mystical convener, they create spaces for comrades to explore & discover who they be individually & collectively. Queerly Complex works with dreams, value(s), structures, & equity to conjure forms of liberation & healing. Queerly Complex art-making centers the messy, intangible, emotive, & esoteric bits that make us human. Find Queerly Complex on Instagram, Twitter, Facebook, and YouTube.

## About The Editor

**Minister James Admans, M.Div. (they/them)** is a preacher, activist, and drag queen residing on the unceded homeland of the Lenape (Lenapehoking), commonly known today as New York City. They are a graduate of Union Theological Seminary in the City of New York where they received their Master of Divinity degree in interdisciplinary Biblical studies, social ethics, and queer theology. In their last year in seminary, James was the recipient of the prestigious Malcolm Boyd Veritas Award for their advocacy and social justice work on behalf of the queer and transgender community.

James currently serves as the Digital Minister at Fort Washington Collegiate Church in the neighborhood of Washington Heights. They work in collaboration with ministers and staff to organize worship, maintain the church's online presence, advance social justice and outreach efforts, and coordinate the small group ministry Beyond Labels. James runs a public queer theology project on Instagram (@theology.queen) and performs and preaches in drag as their alter-ego Marge Erin Johnson (she/her).

## Other Riverdale Titles You Might Like

***TRANS/Gressive:***
***How Transgender Activists Took on Gay Rights, Feminism, the Media and Congress***
By Riki Wilchins

***Burn the Binary***
By Riki Wilchins

***Read My Lips:***
***Sexual Subversion and the End of Gender***
By Riki Wilchins

***Queer Theory, Gender Theory: And Instant Primer***
By Riki Wilchins

***Hiding in Plain Sight***
By Zane Thimmesch-Gill

***Finding Masculinity:***
***Female to Male Transition in Adulthood***
Edited by Alexander Walker and Emmett J.P. Lundberg

***Outside the XY:***
***Queer, Black and Brown Masculinity***
Edited by Brooklyn Boihood

***Queering Sexual Violence:***
***Radical Voices from Within the Anti-Violence Movement***
Edited by Jennifer Patterson

www.ingramcontent.com/pod-product-compliance
Lightning Source LLC
Chambersburg PA
CBHW030727150426
42813CB00051B/318
*9781626016392*